The Potato Peeler

By Paul P Rachmanides

PublishAmerica
Baltimore

Prologue

It was a spellbinding moment for me. Observing a bright star streaking across the night sky, from west to east, only to disappear in five minutes. It was a US satellite.

My imagination escaped the narrow confines of my environment where I was born and grew up. My mind's eye would travel halfway around the world, trying to learn what makes America capable of so many incredible achievements. Mesmerized and in awe, I had the audacity to dare by promising myself that one day I would make America my home. The year was 1963 and I was 13 years old.

On August 23, 1971, I arrived in the United States without knowing a word of English or anyone. Getting a student VISA was a near miracle.

Dreaming big, relentless, tenacity, stamina, sacrifice and suffering are all prerequisite to success. Finally, I believe "he who dares wins".

Perhaps, this is what W.E. Channing had in mind when he wrote his famous quote: "Perhaps it's what you must have in mind when you take that next step into the unknown, when you dare to live."

Chapter 1: The Family Tree

On November 19, 1949, Dimitrios and Vasiliki Rahmanidis welcomed the arrival of their much anticipated child, a boy, and named him Panteleimon or Pantelis for short. Pantelis was their second child, the first one died in her crib seven years earlier. My parents couldn't do enough for me, I was told much later by neighbors and relatives. My sister Dina arrived in 1951 and my brother George in 1953.

I was born and grew up in Dikea, Eyros, Greece, a town of about 1,500 people located about four miles north of where Greece, Turkey and Bulgaria meet. Eyros is the biggest river in Greece and also serves as a boundary with Bulgaria & Turkey. My hometown is situated on the west bank of the river, but the east bank belongs to Bulgaria. On the Bulgarian side guards were stationed on tall towers, about half a mile from each other, ready to shoot at anyone who would dare to escape to the Greek side. From time to time we could see tracers illuminating the area at night and hear gunfire, clear evidence that someone was trying to escape. The Iron curtain was real and in front of us.

The majority of Dikea residents emigrated from Topolograf, Bulgaria in 1920. At that time, Greece and Bulgaria agreed to a population exchange with the river Eyros to be the dividing line. This meant that the Greek people living in Bulgaria could emigrate to Greece and Bulgarians living in Greece could move to Bulgaria. My grandparents of both sides decided to move to Greece. As soon as they crossed the river Eyros they decided to stay put and make the town of Dikea their homestead.

The Home Environment

Farming and raising cattle was the main occupation of most families, including both of my grandparents. It was a tough life and a difficult one to make ends meet. Despite the difficulty, both of my grandparents managed to do well and accumulate a substantial wealth in terms of farming acreage and heads of cattle.

My father was the 3rd out of four brothers and was born in Topolograf, Bulgaria on April 20th, 1920. My mom was born in 1921 in Dikea, Greece. She had three brothers and three sisters. In 1938 my father's father underwent a stomach surgery in Athens and died from complications. Right after that, the older two brothers each grabbed a quarter of my grandfather's wealth and went their separate ways. The youngest brother was prone to sickness, so my grandmother told my father that if he stayed and took care of her and helped raise the younger brother, my father would be entitled to half the wealth that was left over. My father agreed.

In 1940, my father was drafted into the army and was sent to fight the Germans in the island of Crete. The German paratroopers eventually overwhelmed the island and my father was captured. For six months, along with other prisoners, he was forced to unload bombs from German ships in the port of Iraklion. Six months into his captivity, he saw an opportunity to escape and he did. It took him another six months journeying through the war ravaged countryside to return home.

Soon after he returned he proposed to my mother and they got married in 1942. From 1946-1949 my father served again in the Greek army fighting Greek communist guerillas. In 1948 he was injured but managed to recover. Early in 1955 he felt he had fulfilled his promise to his mother and decided that it was time for him to go his own way. By that time he and his wife had three kids aged six, four and two years old. He had spent thirteen years taking care of his mother and younger brother.

The separation was a traumatic one. This was one of my first recollections of my young life. My grandmother reneged on her agreement and insisted the remaining half of my grandfather's wealth be divided by three between her, my father and his younger brother. Both older brothers came over to our side of the house to demand that my father accepts a third of the wealth, not a half as promised. At one point the oldest brother lunged towards my father to hit him. I vividly remember yelling "Daddy" and crying. At the end he ended up with less than a third and fell into a deep depression. Afterwards he disappeared for several days. My mom was anxious and often crying, my two siblings were too young to understand, so as the oldest I felt I had to do something and decided to go look for my dad.

One late afternoon, without telling my mom, I left the house and started walking towards the direction I last saw my dad was headed. Our house was at the edge of the town so within minutes I was out in the open countryside. Far away I saw a human silhouette moving towards me but I could not tell who that person was so I increased my pace hoping it was my father. Finally I recognized him and started running towards him. When we met, my father with an apprehensive look said, "Panteloud (short for little Pantelis) what are you doing here, so far from the house?"

"To look for you, dad. I don't want to be without a dad."

A frozen grin appeared on his face and said "Don't worry, you will not be without a dad. Now, let's go home." Holding my hand, father and son headed home. It was one of the earliest and happiest memories of my life.

But life was about to get tough for me. We had two cows but no stable, a few chickens and a few acres of farmland and no brick oven to bake bread. Within a year my father built a stable and an oven by making his own bricks. It was backbreaking work. In a spot about a mile outside the town he would make many wooden molds in the form of a brick, then fill them up with mud and let them dry in order to firm up. When he had made enough of them he started to make a stack about thirty feet wide and thirty feet deep and ten feet high. Each layer of dry mud bricks was separated by about two inches of coal. As he was stacking the bricks, he would simultaneously construct a containment wall out of real bricks on the outer perimeter of the stack. Then, he would light the coal and the whole stack would turn into a furnace for about a week. Then, he would take out the outer wall so the stack could cool off. His next step was to transfer the ready bricks to our back yard where the stable and oven would be built. All that took place in the summer where the summer heat and subsequent perspiration would at times become unbearable. Of course, I was part of this process by helping with minor chores.

Farming was done the old way by plowing the land with a pair of cows and hand picking the crop. Mechanization was nonexistent in the late 50's, it did not arrive in my hometown until the early 60's. Grain was the main crop and local farmers would sell their grain to the co-op. Some years would be good and some bad, so we were barely able to survive.

But my life did not get tough for me because of hard work or getting by with just a few things. My father became very strict with me. He was telling me that he was strict with me for my own good, to instill in me principles that would help me grow up the right way, by following instructions to the letter. Principles like working hard, be conservative with money (don't spend a dime without a good reason), be honest and always tell the truth the first time. Pick good people as your friends and avoid the bad ones. He loved telling me "Tell me who your friends are and I will tell you who you are".

He thought if he would be strict with me my younger siblings would get the message and he wouldn't have to work on them as hard. My father had a temper. He believed the quickest and most effective way to instill these principles was through physical punishment, like slapping me in the face or hitting me on my back with a thin, flexible branch that left half a dozen red lines and was very painful. My mother was the peacemaker, many times she wouldn't talk to my father for weeks. At one time he threatened to hang me. I thought of running away, but where to? I knew that eventually he would catch up with me and then he would hang me for sure.

I was probably nine years old when my father asked me to meet him in the front yard of our house. I was a bit tense, but I noticed he was smiling, a rare event. "I heard you are telling your mother that I don't love you because I am too strict with you. You are wrong, I love you very much but you're too young to understand. I know you would like to have a little room to wiggle, to do what you want to do, live like some other kids do, but I don't care about them I only care about you. Until you become eighteen years old you will follow my instructions and I don't care if you like them or not. Once you get to be eighteen years old you can do whatever you want, I will not interfere."

Boy, I thought, I can't wait to become eighteen. Then he asked me "Look at our front yard, what do you see?"

I said "I see trees."

"Which one do you like?"

I thought, is this a trick question? "That one," I said.

"Why?"

"Because it grew straight up, like a candle. "

"Hm.. why didn't you pick the one your grandmother planted, it is much bigger than the one you picked."

"Well dad, its trunk and branches are all crooked, it doesn't look good."

"Very good son. The tree that you like, it was thin and fragile when I planted it but I tied it to a pole so the wind would not deform its development. I took the pole out when the tree grew strong enough to withstand the push and pull of the wind. The discipline on you is the pole that you must be tied to until you become eighteen years old. When my mother planted her tree, the one you don't like, she did not tie it to a pole."

"Oh, now I understand dad." Suddenly, all this punishment didn't hurt as much.

Chapter 2: Escaping the Gravity of my Strict Environment

In the summer of 1959, at the age of ten, I got a job at the co-op. The person in charge was the brother—in-law of my Godfather. He agreed, at my father's request, to let me work there as a gofer with no pay so I could get exposure to the real world. My duties included sweeping the floors and bringing, from a nearby coffee shop, coffee, sodas and cigarette packs to the people who were actually running the place. These people were government employees, all of them high school graduates and held in high esteem. Some of them would come to work with the daily newspaper and others with their subscribed magazines. So every time I had nothing to do I attempted to read them. In doing so my reading skills improved, but the real benefit was that my mind burst the narrow confines of my birth place. Up to that point the boundary of my whole world was marked by the visible horizon around me, and half of it belonged to Bulgaria.

At first, I started learning about events taking place inside Greece, then events outside Greece near and far and eventually I learned of events taking place around the world. My curiosity piggybacked my mind and my imagination and soon I was traveling to foreign lands and wanted to know more. What a wonderful escape! Into that state of mind I would find excitement, calmness, security and promise. The summer of 1960 was more of the same.

My Middle and High School Years

Neither of my parents went to high school so they were determined that all three of their children would go. I was scheduled to finish the 6'th grade in June of 1961. It meant that I would have to attend middle school in the city some 60 kilometers away. My sister and my brother were following me by two and four years respectively. That would be an expense that farming could not support. My father came to the realization that the only way he could support us was for him to go and work in West Germany as a guest worker. At that time West Germany was in need of foreign workers and many of my town's people found work there.

In June of 1961 my father left for West Germany and that was like my 4th of July—a heavy load was lifted off my shoulders as I celebrated my freedom. The Greek Government approved, in the summer of 1961, the establishment of a middle school in my hometown and scrambled to staff the faculty. I attended middle school in my hometown. Severely understaffed and under-funded, we had no foreign language teacher.

My interest in the world outside Greece continued. I had developed the habit of reading newspapers and magazines about the NASA program, including the sub-orbital flight of Alan Shepard and the first space flight by John Glenn, throughout my middle and high school years. I remember the moment when Sputnik went into space on October 4, 1957 but it was the American space program of the early 60s that captured my imagination. By listening to the radio and reading the newspapers, I knew when a rocket would blast off from Cape Canaveral. Every night of a launch I would get on top of a hill and gaze at the sky. Then, a bright star would appear on the western horizon moving towards the eastern horizon and would disappear in about five minutes. By now, my friends and classmates realized that I kept up with current events outside Greece, so when President Kennedy got assassinated I was asked by some of them "Who killed Kennedy?" I replied that I didn't know at the moment, but I would find out and let them know.

The government, in the summer of 1964, approved the founding of a high school in my hometown. Like the middle school it had barebones faculty staffing and still no foreign language teacher. As the years were passing by, my desire to go to America was growing, but I kept it to myself. In the early spring of 1967, our teachers were encouraging us to pick a subject and make a presentation to the whole student body. I gave a presentation about the American space program. In late June of 1967 I graduated from high school. Every year since 1962 my father would come home for one month. His attitude had changed, he showed a softer side and he acted like a guest.

In the summer of 1967 he came back and stayed for almost a year, recuperating from an ulcer of the stomach surgery he underwent in West Germany. The doctors took out three-quarters of his stomach. While he was at home, he tried several times to entice me to join him in West Germany. He would describe the German society as a perfect one. Industrious, disinclined, clean, orderly, well organized, progressive, an excellent health care system and going to the university was virtually free. Besides, he would be right there to help me out with whatever I needed. Boy, the thought to be under his influence again gave me chills. I wanted to get away, far far away from everybody, especially from him. I wanted a total and absolute freedom to do whatever I would decide to do with my life. Of course, I said none of the above to my father. Instead, I thanked him for the nice offer and sheepishly briefly mentioned to him that I was contemplating of going to America to attend the university there.

His jaw dropped, "But you don't know the language or anybody there. I hear that you have to pay to attend the university and it is very expensive, why would you want to go to America and not come to Germany with me where education is free?"

"But that's where I want to go dad."

"Well son, now you are old enough to decide for yourself. I will not interfere with your plans. Just remember that whatever you do in your life you will not do it for me or for your mother but for yourself. I will help you though, as much as I can."

"Thank you dad, that's all I need." Shortly after that he left for Germany again.

My best friend Thanasis and I were the only ones, from our graduating class of 12, that didn't rush to get career jobs. He knew he would become a customs agent but only after completing his two year military duty. In Greece, at the time, every man served for two years. As for myself, I was holding back. I was hesitant to embark in a certain direction only to find out later that I chose the wrong one and lead a life of regret and unfulfilled promise. I wanted to be absolutely, positively sure that whatever direction I took it was the right one. I wanted to never doubt, regret or complain about my choice no matter what difficulties, sacrifices or impossible odds I would be forced to endure. But how can you find a golden needle in a haystack the first time you try?

Well, how about following the process of elimination. For several months I would run the following imaginary test. I would pick a job and then run an imaginary life that job would offer me. I repeated this process with dozens of jobs. None of them satisfied me and most of them gave me the creeps. I would then imagine coming to America and I would feel goose bumps all over my body, tears in my eyes and a slight trembling. "That's it," I said, "I found it and that's what I am going to do." That was the easy part as long as those thoughts were in my head. But the time had arrived to let family and relatives know what I was thinking of doing.

During the second half of 1967, my relatives were nudging me to do something, to move, to get a job (any job), like my classmates so I could get a career going. When I finally told them that I wanted to go to America they had a field day. They put me down in every way they could, calling me a lazy, procrastinating daydreamer gazing at the pie in the sky. The more they pressured me the more determined I became, and then I would withdraw into my mental cocoon.

My best friend and I were working in construction during the day and would hang out at night with two other friends of ours. One was the manager of the phone company and the other was serving his military duty as a Second Lieutenant in the National Guard. We would hang out almost every night and drink and smoke a pack a day. We talked about life, girls, careers and especially politics. The officer and the manager both laughed when I first told them about my plans. They told me that both of them passed the TOFEL examination and were accepted by American universities, but both were denied a student VISA because many more qualified people applied for a student VISA than the quota would allow.

"You, my friend" they said to me, "do not meet the most basic requirement—you don't know a word of English! Take our advice and forget about America. Don't let your hopes get too high because the higher you fly the harder you would crash. When that happens, and we guarantee it will happen, please don't think that it is the end of the world. We thought so too for a while, but we compromised and adjusted into a new reality and you will too."

Compromise is the word I hate most when it is time to choose your direction in life. It is devoid of hope, lacking a chance for the better and it denotes stagnation which leads to living in a rut. A life without meaning, living as a breathing dead.

I got a bit deflated and depressed, I felt the enormity of my undertaking and the impossible odds that I was facing. It was a reality check to see two live examples who went through this path before me and both were significantly more qualified than me, yet were unable to achieve their dream. I couldn't let my purpose in life, my prize, to slip away. By now it became a force, a burning desire and a purpose worth living for and I intended to pursue it relentlessly.

I had to respond to them. "I know you are my friends, thank you for your encouragement but I don't need it." I find encouragement from within, and promptly placed their experience in the back of my head on the backburner, to serve as a constant reminder of the difficulties lying ahead, but I remained determined to forge ahead towards my goal.

In the summer of 1968 I applied at the Greek Military Academy and took a series of tests. I was denied entrance, math and science were my weak points. In contrast, political science, history, geography and current affairs were my forte. Early on, I was able to obtain a clear and accurate snapshot of the Greek political and economic landscape and I didn't like what became apparent. A person like me with my kind of background, inclination and goal in life didn't have much of a chance for upward movement. I felt that the system was constrained, inflexible and unnecessarily divided. There were two major parties in Greece and they were diametrically opposed. One was inching towards western style democracy and the other had a socialistic agenda in its purest form. So, the party in power at the moment was shutting out the other. Representatives were voting strictly on party lines. There was no compromise and no cooperation. On the other hand, the opposition party was claiming that the party in power was doing nothing right. So when the tables were turned in the next election, the first priority of the party in power was to undo what the previous government achieved. It was a sad situation rife with inaction, nasty bickering and yes there were elections but no real progress. In April 1967 a military coup took power to restore order.

By the time I got out of high school in June of 1967 I had a clear picture of the political, economic and social landscape of Greece. I was thinking that there must be a better way of doing things, in a different place, by different people. So, I decided to pick a place outside Greece and make it my home. I would have a second birthday, a conscious one. I would grow up in a different culture, learn a different language and learn to participate and assimilate into their political, economic and social system. I would become one of them. But where to? Which country must I choose and make sure it is the right one for me. I had to come up with some kind of litmus test.

I was aware that all foreign languages were difficult to learn and the assimilation would also be difficult. So, I concluded that the Litmus test would be: "At the end, would it all be worth it? Would the country I choose be worth the sacrifice and effort I would have to endure?" I also knew that your point of view depended on where you stand. Since I was born and grew up in an environment with a somewhat restrictive vantage point of the world, by the fact that I was looking from the bottom upwards so, I was wondering as to how the world would look like if, my vantage point would allow me to look at the world from top to bottom. At the time there were only two peaks, the Soviet Union and America, and who in his right mind would want to go to the Soviet Union. I said to myself, America in less than 200 years became a superpower, and put men on the moon, and safely brought them back. They must be doing something right. I need to go there and find out what they are doing right, what makes them tick.

Chapter 3: The Military Experience

The nagging of my relatives continued until March of 1969. Next month, in April, I was drafted into the Army. Thank God I got away from everybody! Everyone with a high school education or higher was reporting to the military base in the city of Corinth. There we would undergo a two month basic training. During that time career officers from different military branches would come in and, after a series of tests, would pick a number of us for intensive five month training. Upon graduation we would become officers on probation with the condition that if we were to satisfactorily perform our duties for a specified period of time then we would become Second Lieutenants. If one wanted to stay and make a career in the military, his chances of moving upward would be the same as a Second Lieutenant coming out of the military academy because performance was a key factor.

The majority of us (I was one of them) were sent to the infantry academy in Iraklion, Crete. About ten days before graduation from the infantry academy, officers from Special Forces (Green Beret) and the Marines came in to do their picking from a class of approximately 350. After a series of tests, the Special Forces officers picked thirty-two cadets and I was one of them.

The senior officer said to us, "We promise you excitement, adventure, intensive training and you will be able to do things that most people think cannot be done. As you know, we accept into our ranks only volunteers. We chose you, now it is time for you to choose us. If any one of you would like to bow out now is the time."

Four cadets raised their hand and were dismissed. We were expected to report four days after graduating from the academy to camp Redina, a Special Forces base in Northern Greece. After a thirty-five day intensive boot camp training, we were assigned to our respective battalions. I, with three others officers joined our Battalion in the mountains in early January 1970.

All four of us returned to Redina in late February 1970 to undergo an eleven week special training called the Ranger school (others call it survival school). Regardless of which name you use, if you could survive that training you could survive anything. On the first day a Captain (the Director of the school) greeted us in a classroom ready to offer us a glimpse of what lied ahead of us in the form of a slideshow. The very first picture that was projected on the screen showed the Captain holding from the neck and the tail a humongous snake.

With a smile on his face he said, "I am tempted to bet that all of you consider this as something to be avoided. Let me assure you that there will come a time when you would consider this a delicacy."

We looked at each other in disbelief. Then, two officers of the class raised their hands and said, "We don't think so, we are bowing out." Thus, our group ended up with 26 officers, all of whom successfully finished the training.

"You," the Captain continued, "will find yourselves operating beyond your perceived limits; you will discover that you possess reserves you didn't know you had. You will develop a character (a cornerstone of it all) and obtain the confidence that with proper preparation and flawless execution nothing is impossible. The first phase of the program will consist of intensive strength training and learning about the fundamentals of special operations in a classroom."

The 8'th week was particularly tough. Let me be specific. We woke up at 5:30 AM on Monday and were supposed to go to bed again the following Saturday. It was called a week of continued action and went like this. Up at 5:30 AM Monday, after having breakfast, we were given an assignment to hit a target on Monday night. So we used the daytime to study, plan, organize and practice the best approach and execution. Three trainers were assigned to our group. Their job was to observe and grade our performance. At specified times the trainer would assign one of us to leadership for a period of time and then assign it to somebody else so, over time each of us would have a chance to lead the group. Each of the three trainers was with us for eight hours, so we were observed 24/7.

Monday night we successfully hit the target and returned to base Tuesday morning. We had breakfast and received a new assignment. We spent all day preparing and hit the target Tuesday night. Same thing on Wednesday, but in the evening of that day we were told by our trainer that because our group was so cohesive and performed so well the captain decided to reward us by canceling that night's hit and allowing us to sleep that night. Thursday morning we were back to the regular program and Friday more of the same. Friday night we hit the wall. Exhaustion and sleep deprivation pushed us into the twilight zone. It was a world I never experienced before and I was amazed that I could still function. That's when I realized what the Captain meant on the first day. On Saturday around 11 AM we got back to base, ate lunch, showered and hit the sack around 2 PM. When I woke up it was Sunday around 4 PM.

Upon graduation mid May of 1970, we received our diplomas and an emblem with the inscription, "He who dares, wins." I rejoined my battalion in the mountains doing a summer reconnaissance of our assigned sector.

My father, in the summer of 1970 was on his way back to West Germany. He stopped by and visited me in Thessaloniki for a few days. He tried again to entice me to join him in West Germany but I refused.

He said "I will help you with money if you manage to go to America. But if some day I tell you I can't help you anymore I will be telling you the truth, so don't depend on me 100%."

I said "Don't worry dad, just help me to set foot over there and I'll take care of things from then on."

We then talked about the early days and he acknowledged that at times he was perhaps too strict but insisted that he meant well. I asked him the following question: "Dad, when you disappeared for several days in 1955, what did you do, where did you go and why did you come back?"

He stared at the floor in deep thought then said "I had spent a couple of nights out in the open countryside debating with myself as to whether I should commit suicide or run away and abandon all of you. Then, it came to me that a good friend of mine in the nearby village had a similar experience with his family so I paid him a visit. We talked all night and at the end he said to me: '**Listen Dimitri, it is not important what you inherit. What is important in life is what YOU, yourself create. The family is a source of strength; take care of your family.**' That advice gave me a huge shot of hope and confidence. I realized that my self-worth cannot be defined by my brothers. So, I decided to come back home for you all and outdo everybody."

On October 30, 1970 I became a paratrooper by making the mandatory five jumps, the last one at night. Then, I went back to the mountains. Let me mention a few things about special operations people. They are secretive, stealthy, self-sufficient, use the element of surprise and they are deadly. They inflict maximum damage in the shortest period of time possible. They prefer to operate at night and observe the target preferably for forty-eight hours but not less than twenty-four for real time intelligence to identify the enemy's weakest point and know the best time to attack. They avoid ravines, mountain ridges, trails and pathways; all of them are death traps. Stealth and the element of surprise is their biggest weapon. If the enemy can't see you they can't hurt you. Motion invites detection, detection turns into vulnerability, vulnerability leads to disadvantage and disadvantage translates into being 50% dead. The other 50% will be determined by the ability of your enemy to pursue you and your ability to escape. You don't want to be in that situation, ever. That is why we stay low during the day and prefer to operate only at night. You never want to let the enemy fight you on a level playing field. You want him to be at an extreme disadvantage, to be off balance. That's what the element of surprise does. They take no prisoners and especially don't let them go free. Finally, they prefer for the enemy to be dead before the enemy realizes what hit him.

Right after I became a paratrooper I was promoted to Second Lieutenant. In early January, 1971 my company was conducting reconnaissance in an area where Greece borders Albania, one of the most mountainous areas in Greece. My platoon covered an area that I found to be very strange. It was an elevated rocky area where half a dozen dry wells were occupying the surface. The wells were about 50 to 60 feet in diameter and about 25 feet deep. It was snowing all night and the area was covered with snow about a foot high. The next morning I walked down to Captain Aristides Palainis' tent to plan the coming night's operation.

I was about an hour into meeting with my Captain when my Corporal walked into the Captain's tent with a tense face and said: "Mr. Rahmanidis, a bear attacked us!"

"Oh God, who is dead?" I asked.

"Nobody," the Corporal replied.

What a relief for me and my Captain. I asked what happened and the Corporal said: "Well, me and the other two spent the night at the spot you sent us. In the morning we wanted to start a bonfire so we started looking for wood and we saw dry branches at the bottom of the dry well. So, two of us started descending into the well. When we got near the bottom a white mass suddenly lunged towards us. I realized it was a bear and I started shooting at her. She got to about four or five steps from us when abruptly she turns to the right and starts climbing the dry well. She disappeared!"

"So, where is the other guy?"

"He is safe, he climbed a tree and is waiting for us to come back."

The Captain turned towards me and said, "Mr. Rahmanidis I want you to pick a few men, go there and bring everybody over here."

"Captain, I ask for permission to descend into the dry well to see if the bear gave birth to cubs, I suspect she did."

"Oh no, I don't want anybody to get hurt."

"Captain, I guarantee no one will get hurt."

"Ok, Mr. Rahmanidis; but if someone gets hurt I will hold you responsible."

"Ok Captain, I accept."

I arrived at the well with six men. First, I wanted to make sure the bear didn't make a U-turn to protect her cubs. So we followed for about half a mile a blood stain on the snow and they appeared to be in a straight line away from the well. We returned to the well and I placed four of my men around the well with orders to shoot the bear if she showed up. I took my sergeant with me down the well as cover. Both of us slowly (and with some apprehension) were approaching the spot where I thought the cubs might be. Sure enough, I saw a shallow cave and three bundles of joy—each about eight inches long. They were making some noise trying to keep warm by constantly covering each other. Quickly, I placed all three in a plastic raincoat and walked away in a hurry. When we got to the surface we placed them close to the fire and took some pictures. The next day we were scheduled to return to our base in the city of Thessaloniki. Within a few days we asked the people at the city zoo to pick up the bear cubs and take care of them.

In April of 1971 I completed my two year military duty and was honorably discharged. When I said goodbye to my captain, Aristides Palainis, he gave me his home phone number and said to me, "Mr. Rahmanidis, in your civilian life, if you think that I can do something for you please don't hesitate to call me, I'll do whatever I can. I am rarely at home and when I am I don't stay for very long but if you keep calling eventually you'll get hold of me."

I responded with, "Thank you Captain, I'll keep this in mind."

Chapter 4: Time for Action

And now I reached the crossroad. The time of thinking, contemplating, wishing, hoping and dreaming was over. The time for action had arrived. What I would be able to do during the next few months would determine whether I would go to America or get stuck in Greece forever, and the latter was giving me the creeps. My whole life, full of promise, was ahead of me and would have been wasted if the latter would have happened. I spent the month of May 1971 in my hometown, digging deep into myself to find out what I was made of, feeling the gravity of my decision and being aware of the overwhelming odds against me.

Pete, my mother's younger brother, was a state bureaucrat and considered to be the educated, wise man of the clan. At my mom's request he came over and took me for a long walk with the specific purpose to instill some good sense into my head. He emphatically stated that he knew all about America and America was not for me.

"You'll never make it," he said. "Americans are industrious, they pull their own weight, and if you don't you will become homeless living under a bridge. People will be passing by and won't even look at you, everybody is for himself. I'm absolutely sure you won't get the VISA, you don't know a word of English and you don't know anybody over there. But let's assume you somehow manage to arrive there. What do you think will happen? A red carpet and drums of a band will be announcing your arrival? You'll end up under a bridge, will steal a loaf of bread because you'll be starving to death, you will be caught, thrown in jail and then get deported. So you can avoid all that by staying here."

He went on, "The English language is very difficult to learn. Americans compress and abbreviate, they speak inside their mouths and they pronounce a word one way but they write it down in another. Let me give you an example. The word Pennsylvania, do you know how they write it down?"

"No Uncle, how?"

"As PA he said, with a smile. Now even if you know the words, which you don't, you wouldn't know how to write them down. In addition, there is grammar and syntax to deal with. You see, you are looking at four levels of difficulty all at once! Do I make sense to you?"

"Yes Uncle Pete but I still want to go."

He was taken aback. He took it personally, he failed and looked at me like he was feeling sorry for me and then he said, "Like Pontius Pilate washed his hands, I also wash my hands from you. I've done my duty and there is nothing else to do, but I'll tell you what. If you somehow manage to get there and learn the language and attend a University I promise you I will do the following. At noon, in the center of the city of Alexandroupolis I will take off all my clothes and I will walk totally naked."

And with that, we parted.

Chapter 5: Getting a Student Visa

In early June, 1971, I flew to Athens and went to the American Embassy. An impressive building on a slope of a hill and a sign that told me I needed to go to the back of the building. I noticed a little window, much like a bank teller would have. I asked the young lady for information on how to go to America. When I told her that I didn't speak a word of English she said "Don't bother, you'll be wasting your time. You'll never get a VISA."

I pleaded with her again and I got the same answer. So, as politely as I could I said to her, "Mam, the time is mine if I want to waste it. I can do that, so would you please give me some information?"

She, with concealed contempt, handed me a one page paper. I took a few steps away from her window and I started reading. *"Ways to Go to the United States"* : If you have a family member who is a US citizen, If you invest a million dollars, If your specialty is needed and over a half a dozen other ways but none of them applied to me. But, at the very bottom of the page I noticed an asterisk with a few lines of a very fine print that stated: "For those of you who would like to go to the United States of America, they can do so if they attend an Intensive English Center that some of the universities provide." Voila! I found the beginning.

I walked back to the window and asked her for the list of universities with an Intensive English Center. She said that I could get the list from the American Library on the 3'rd floor on a central street near downtown Athens. I took a taxi to the library and climbed the stairs three at a time.

When I got to the 3'rd floor a sweet, young lady said "May I help you?"

"Yes, a list of universities that also have an Intensive English Center?"

She said, "I assume you know some of the English language?"

"No mam, I don't."

"Oh, then you are wasting your time."

"Mam, the time is mine to waste." At that moment she started turning her head to her left and I followed her by turning mine to the right. An older lady, with glasses and white hair (just like the church lady on Saturday Night Live) who was listening, nodded her head to the young lady in the affirmative. Within a few minutes the young lady came back with one page of information.

The same day I flew to Thessaloniki where a friend of mine was a junior at the Greek University and was taking English classes. When I got to his apartment he offered me a new soft drink from America. I said "Oh, it is like a 7up!"

He said "No no, it is a Sprite!"

He asked me to write in Greek what I wanted to say and he tried to translate it into English. He suggested that his English professor needed to polish it, which she did the next day and then he copied it six times and asked me to sign them. He was amazed when I told him I don't know how. Then, he printed my name on a paper and I copied it letter by letter.

While I was waiting to hear from the American Universities I visited an old classmate of mine whose mother came to Thessaloniki to visit him. She was well known in my hometown as the lady who can look at an inverted cup of Greek coffee and tell you about events in your past, present and future. So, they offered me Greek coffee and afterwards asked me to shake it and then invert the cup. The lady, while looking at my coffee cup, said, "Pantelis, I see a long trip ahead of you. You are going to run into many obstacles but you will overcome them. A group of people are waiting for you, it looks like a family."

Right then I interrupted her in jest saying, "Oh no, you mean the Mafia is waiting for me?"

"No, no, no Pantelis, these people mean well for you. They will take you under their wing and they will be a Godsend to you. I see one, two, three, four, five people who are just waiting for you."

I thought, "She knows I am trying to go to America and she is trying to offer me some encouragement." I thanked her and promptly dismissed the event.

The University of Kansas and the University of Michigan replied positively. But the University of Michigan was $1500 more expensive than Kansas so I decided to go to Kansas. The University of Kansas sent me some papers and the address of the bus depot in Kansas City, along with the times of departure to Lawrence. 10:30 PM was the last bus to leave. The letter also stated that I must report my arrival to the Dean of Foreign Students no later than August 24th to be allowed to attend the fall semester at the Intensive English Center.

In late July of 1971, I went to the American Consulate in Thessaloniki to apply for a student VISA. The Consul, a tall blonde and slender man named John Peters heard me carefully and then informed me through a young female translator that he was sorry for having to turn me down.

"Because of the quota system the Consul cuts 4 out of 5 qualified applicants and you do not meet the basic requirement of knowing the language. You are looking for adventure. You may go now."

I was shaken. When I got outside, I saw dark clouds and I said to myself, "That's strange, it was a bright sunny day half an hour ago. I was feeling light headed and a bit unstable, and car horns were going off all over the place. Had I drifted into the traffic and was I going to faint?

I tried to move as close to the building as I could, thinking, "If I am going to faint at least I'll drop on the sidewalk and not in the middle of traffic." In a few minutes, the dark clouds disappeared and the day became bright and shiny again. Then I started walking back to my room.

It was the most sad, depressed and hopeless walk of my life. I fell into a deep depression. I could not eat, sleep or talk to anyone. I lost 6 kilos in 11 days. My heart and mind had already arrived in the United States and was imagining how I would like life to be. All that remained to be done was simply transport my body over there. Instead, the American Consul dropped an iron curtain in front of me that said "you can't go there". Well, I am a person who does not take no for an answer.

I would take walks for several hours in one direction just to keep my mind from going crazy. My friends in the past had warned me that this would happen but I could not accept it. I couldn't see myself getting stuck in Greece. Slowly my system was starting to shut down. I was getting weaker and weaker by the day. To me, America was a magnet and it was not defined merely by Mexico, Canada, and the Atlantic and Pacific Oceans. America is a state of mind on a global scale. It is a place where anything is possible, a land full of promise, it is the promise land and I had to get there.

Then, one day late in the afternoon around August 10th, what my Captain told me came to my mind. So I rushed to my room and picked up his home phone number. I walked into the first phone booth I could find and dialed the Captain.

I was holding my breath when he answered, "Aristides Palainis here, who is calling?"

"Captain, this is Pantelis Rahmanidis."

"Mr. Rahmanidis, how are you?"

"Fine Captain, but I have a problem."

"Oh, what is it?"

I went on to explain my situation to him. "Captain, as you know I want to go to America and the Consul turned me down. I am at a loss, I don't know what to do."

Silence. Then, "Mr. Rahmanidis, I don't know anybody in the American Consulate. In addition, Americans don't like us because we have a junta government and I certainly can't walk into his office and put a gun to his head and make him give you the VISA."

I thought, "Oh God, I've ran into a dead end again."

The Captain interrupted my thoughts. "Why don't you go back again, Mr. Rahmanidis?"

My ears started buzzing. He couldn't possibly mean go back to the American Consulate. "Go back where, Captain?"

"Back to the Consulate and talk to the Consul again."

"But Captain, I haven't learned the English language during the last two weeks, so what am I going to tell him?"

"Ahhhh, Mr. Rahmanidis, that's your problem!" This made my mind feel like it was inside a black box and I was headed down for a crash.

The Captain then said, "Just because he said no the first time it doesn't mean that he will say no the second time. For him to say yes or no is the same thing. So far you gave him a reason to say no. Listen to me, I spent some time in America both as a civilian and for military training. I have a pretty good grasp of their culture. **Americans are flexible, they appreciate persistence**."

As soon as I heard the phrase 'Americans are flexible', the black box of my mind cracked just a bit and a ray of hope hit me in the eye. The darkness of the black box I was trapped in started to fade. I was coming back to life and getting back my bearings, realizing that I may not crash after all. I still had time to fight. **Flexibility**, that's where **hope resides**. If you are inflexible, you become stiff and stiff is another word for dead.

Fast forward a couple of decades: *It finally dawned on me that this is the reason the United States is so stable. The system is flexible by allowing constant input from its members. That produces hope, meaning people feel that their opinion matters and they can have an impact on the system. It is a form of government from the bottom up "We the people" as the corner stone of it all. This form of government allows people to vent off their frustrations, gives them hope to improve themselves and promotes cooperation. It is a dynamic, well oiled and amazingly well-functioning organism. It accepts small changes on a regular basis and adapts accordingly. Unlike other parts of the world where the system of government is top to bottom and nothing changes for centuries. So, people's frustrations boil to a point where the only way for change is a violent one.*

The Captain interrupted my thoughts again. "How long is your hair?" he asked.

I looked left and right and said, "Almost touching my shoulders."

"Hhmm, what clothes did you wear?"

"Corduroy pants and shirt, no tie. I thought looking like an American would improve my chances."

The Captain continued with his advice. "What you need to do is this: Get a short hair cut. Press your best three piece suit and wear a tie. Shine your best shoes. Look at him in the eye when you talk to him and don't talk more than ten minutes. By the way, you must be the first one he sees in the morning. In the morning, people are in a good mood. But if he sees you later on in the day, he might be pissed off about something else and take it out on you."

"I got it Captain, thank you very much."

Now I had a plan. I got a short hair cut, I pressed my suit and shirt, got my tie and shined my best shoes and sat at my table. It was 9 PM. I quickly realized that the only subject I could talk to the Consul about was my military experience. I wrote nothing down, instead working on my presentation in my head. At 11:30 PM I clocked at thirty-five minutes.

"Oh no," I thought. "I can't cut anything because all is important! But the Captain said no more than ten minutes.."

At 1 AM I clocked my speech down to twenty minutes. I cut, rephrased and compressed and by 3 AM I brought it down to 9 minutes.

"Perfect," I said, and from 3 to 5 AM I was repeating my 9 minute speech over and over again. I thought if my mind went blank, my mouth would spit the words out.

At 5 AM, I felt that I was ready and I felt a bit tired but definitely didn't want to lie down on the bed. Sitting at my chair, I put my arms on the table and let my head rest on my arms. Suddenly, I jumped up and began desperately looking for my watch. I was worrying I had overslept and lost my chance to be the first in line. Finally, I see my watch—and the time is only 6 AM on the dot! What a relief! I rushed into the shower. After my shower, I got dressed up and ran out the door. I arrived at the Consulate at 6:50 AM and there was no one there but me. By 7:30 AM a line of about thirty people had formed.

At 8:30 AM the doors opened and we were asked to come in. Inside were about thirty chairs put in a half circle formation. I was asked to stand in front of the first chair and the second person in front of the second chair and so on until everyone was inside. I was still standing up when a short, baldheaded guy with an armful of papers walked out of his office and passes in front of me. He passed me by about four steps and freezes. He backed up and stopped in front of me, looking up at me (He was about 5'8" and I am 6'3).

He said, "Weren't you here about two weeks ago and aren't you the one who wants to go to America but don't speak a word of English?"

"Yes sir, I am."

"Have you learned English?"

"No sir, I have not."

"Then, what are you doing here?"

"I want to talk to the Consul again." He gave me a very strange look, rolled his eyes in disbelief and left. Then, we were asked to sit down in our respective chairs.

Within two minutes the door of the Consul's office opened and the same pretty young interpreter looked at me and said, "Will the first one please come in."

I stood up, buttoned my coat and two steps before I stepped into his office I nailed my eyes on the Consul. He was standing up but looking down at his desk. When I got close enough for him to see me, it took him several seconds to recognize me. When he did, his eyes brightened and his head jerked slightly backwards, surprised to see me. He cracked half a smile. I interpreted his reaction that he finally recognized me but couldn't believe the change in my physical appearance.

He greeted me in broken Greek and said "I understand more Greek than I can speak. Please, speak slowly and clearly. If I don't understand something I will simply ask the interpreter. Please sit down."

The Consul's desk was huge, his armchair looked like an emperor's chair to me, projecting clout and power. I noticed a yellow pad and a pencil were laying on his desk right in front of him. At the beginning of my presentation he was looking at me by sitting back on his chair. Towards the middle, he leaned forward with his left elbow on his desk and the other on his armchair. Now he began looking at me from a 45 degree angle. When I finished (precisely at 9 minutes), he picked up his pencil. His head rested on his left arm with his left elbow on the table, and in the top-right corner of the yellow pad he drew four very short lines, all four of them intersecting with each other exactly in the middle.

He put his pencil down and said, "You did not mention your military experience the last time you were here." Then, he pulled his drawer, picked up a piece of paper and looked at me.

"I am holding the deposit receipt from your previous visit of $1250 that your father deposited with Chase Manhattan. If you bring me another receipt showing that your father deposited an additional $1000, which will be enough to cover your expenses for your first year in the United States, I will seriously consider granting you a student VISA."

As soon as he said that I knew what was standing between me and a student VISA was an additional $1000. I knew my father would rob a bank if he had to, to send it to me. I sent an express letter to him asking to deposit an additional $1000 to the Chase Manhattan bank. He was in the hospital when my letter arrived. A cable had broken at his workplace (Mercedez-Bens in Stuttgart) and smashed his big toe. My mother's brother was working in the same city as my father along with many other relatives. He was checking my father's mail for him, and when he saw my letter he brought it to my father in the hospital.

The doctor refused to release him but my father said to the doctor, "My son needs me right now and I am walking out of the hospital with or without your permission. I will sign any papers that you want." He signed a paper that said the doctor would not be responsible if something happened to him.

Within eight days I received the $1000 receipt! It was late in the afternoon on Wednesday, August 18, 1971. The next day at about 10:30 AM I walked into the Consul's office and handed him the deposit receipt. He then called someone in English and someone came in from the adjacent office. It was the guy who a week earlier had rolled his eyes at me. The Consul gave him some instructions and then the assistant motioned at me to follow him to the adjacent office. His desk was cluttered with papers. He picked up a stamp and started pushing and shuffling the papers on his desk.

I was filled with excitement, thinking, "Is he looking for an ink box to stamp my VISA!?"

He found it, turned towards me and asked "Did you bring your passport with you?"

"Yes sir, here it is."

He took it, flipped a few pages and pressed the stamp in the ink box and then applied it onto my passport, then handed it back to me. He looked at me with a look of part bewilderment and part amazement.

He said, "The Consul granted you a four year student VISA with multiple entries into the United States. The norm is just one year. He has never done this before."

When I got outside, I started jumping up and down with joy, yelling, "Yah! I got it!" After a few seconds, I stopped and noticed half a dozen people staring at me intensely. Their facial expression said that they thought I had just flipped.

I looked at each of them in the eye and said, "You probably think I'm crazy, but I assure you I am not. Today is the happiest day of my life. I got the VISA, I am going to America."

And with that I started walking back to my room. I made sure that I followed exactly the same route that I took earlier, I wanted to erase the previous sad walk with this happy one.

The next day, Friday August 20th 1971, I left Thessaloniki and headed back to my hometown. I arrived at our house at 11 PM. My mother was living alone and was asleep so I knocked on the window.

"Oh, it's you son, you came to visit me?"

"Well, yes and no."

"What do you mean no?"

"I came to say goodbye to you mom."

"Why, did you get the VISA?"

"Yeah mom, I am going to America."

"When?"

"Tomorrow morning."

Right then I saw an expression on her face similar to one when a person is standing on the edge of a cliff with her back facing the void and losing her balance, falling into the void. I saw tears in her eyes and she said to me, "Please my son, tell me it's not true. It's OK to lie to me just for tonight, I need to make it through the night."

"No mom, I can't lie to you. I've got to do what I decided to do, just wish me well."

"I wished that your decision and my wish would be the same but since it is not and this is your life I pray to God to keep an eye on you and protect you in the far, foreign land."

I didn't get much sleep that night and I doubt my mom did either. In the morning, as my mom and I were approaching the train station on foot, I said, "Mom, there is an unusually large crowd at the station."

"These people are our relatives, I let them know early in the morning that the train leaves at 9:30 AM and they wanted to say goodbye to you."

Now it is Saturday, August 21, 1971. I must be in Lawrence, Kansas by the 24th and still didn't have an airfare ticket. The possibility of missing my deadline scared me but I had to make it, I had to push forward. At 2:30 PM I took off from Alexandroupolis and arrived in Athens around 4:30 PM.

I flagged a taxi and asked the driver if he could take me to a travel agent so I could buy an airplane ticket to America. He said that he knew someone who sometimes stayed pretty late on Saturdays. He got me there pretty quick and told me the travel office was on the second floor. I ran up and looked at the long, quiet hallway. At that very moment I heard the creaking sound of a door being opened and an elderly man came out and put his hand in his pocket. He took a key out and placed it in the keyhole. I ran towards him and asked him if he was a travel agent. When he said he was, I begged him to help me out.

I needed to buy an airfare for America and leave next Monday. He said that his wife was waiting for him and he was already late for dinner. He said it was impossible because there was not enough time, the flight is booked and that I should come back on Monday. I wanted to hear none of that. I told him that my life depended on me getting the airfare right now and leave for America on Monday.

Reluctantly he unlocked the door and said, "Let me see what I can do."

After an hour of phone calls in his office he said, "Someone canceled his trip to America and we can buy it."

I felt elation, joy and pure ecstasy. At 11:45 AM on Monday, August 23rd, 1971 I left Athens for Chicago via Montreal.

Chapter 6: Arriving in America

Athens to Montreal was a non-stop flight. The plane got refueled and took off for Chicago O'Hare. It was late in the afternoon when the Captain announced that in a few minutes we would be entering the airspace of the United States.

At that very moment the man sitting exactly behind me, a Greek American from Chicago, tapped me on the shoulder and asked me, "Is this your first time to America?"

I felt like Neil Armstrong would have felt if, as soon as he landed on the moon, someone would have asked him, "Is this your first time to the moon?" It was surreal.

In Chicago, I had one hour from touchdown to takeoff. After I went through Immigration and Naturalization Services I searched the signs for the letters "TWA", focusing like the six-million man. I thought I saw the letters and started running towards them. When I found the TWA office I walked inside. My airfare to Kansas City was already paid for, I just needed to get a seat. A young girl with a smile said something to me so I put my passport and other papers on the counter. She realized that I didn't speak English so she talked to the man behind me—an Air Force guy—and motioned with her hand that I needed to follow the Air Force guy. I did and we got to the gate at 7:40 PM Chicago time. The plane took off at 8 PM and shortly after 9 PM we were touching down in Kansas City.

I was holding one small suitcase and scanning the crowd to find a police officer to ask how I could get to the bus depot. "Well," I thought, "a man with a uniform and a gun must be a policeman." I spotted someone with this description who was close to the glass wall, apparently looking from inside out. I approached him from behind and stood there for a minute, hoping to get his attention. Finally, I tapped his left shoulder. He jumped and turned 180' facing me, his face red and full of anger. He was saying something but I couldn't understand. I slowly handed him the little piece of paper showing the bus depot address and the bus timetable, the last bus leaving for Lawrence was at 10:30 PM.

Realizing my situation, he smiled at me and said, "France? Germany?"

I said "Greece."

"Ah, Athens good. Kifisia good." Kifisia is an upper-class suburb of Athens.

He then pressed both of my shoulders with his hands indicating that I shouldn't move but should stay put. I nodded to indicate that I understood.

He returned five minutes later with another guy, also in uniform but his uniform was yellow. The officer said something to the yellow guy. All three of us walked outside and stepped behind a big yellow car. The yellow guy opened the trunk, took my suitcase and very gently placed it inside then went around me and held the rear door open. He motioned for me to get into the back seat. Impressed by the treatment of such polite people I said to myself, "I made the right decision, I already like this place." As soon as we took off I noticed the cab meter, that's when I realized I was in a taxi.

The cab driver did not turn the meter on. When we arrived at the bus depot I extended my hand to him holding a $20, a $10, a $5 and 5 ones. He looked at me in the eye and very slowly pulled two one dollar bills. I motioned to him to take some more money but he refused. Instead, with both of his hands he folded mine, then motioned that I should put my money in my pocket. I thought that would be it and he would take off, but instead he guided me into the bus depot and stayed in line with me until we reached the counter. He helped me buy a bus ticket for Lawrence, and then showed me behind which overhead door my bus was parked. He talked to the bus driver and showed me using his watch that my bus would be leaving at 10:30 pm, then left. It was just before 10 PM. I sat down on the bench and I dozed off. Someone shook me up, it was the bus driver, indicating that it was time for me to get on the bus.

We arrived at the bus depot in downtown Lawrence at about 11 PM Central time. I had fallen asleep during the bus ride, so the driver woke me up and motioned for me to leave the bus. I was the last passenger to get off the bus and by the time I did, I saw three dark complexion, loud speaking young people had already gotten off the bus and were headed for the sidewalk. Even though I didn't know English I could tell they were from the Middle East.

"They must be students coming to the university just like me." I thought.

When I caught up with them a cab had just pulled up next to them. I used my hands to ask them if I could get into the cab with them. They motioned to me that it was ok to get in the cab with them, so I joined them. I didn't know where we were going. They seemed to have made some advanced arrangements and I was willing to crash for the night at the same hotel. The cab pulled in front of a seven story building where the face of the building was full with rows of windows. I thought that it looked like a good hotel. I followed them inside where a young man talked briefly to them and gave them each a key. Then, he asked me something. I nodded and he also gave me a key. I tried to pay but he refused. Two of the guys received a key for room #629 and I was given the key for room #630.

When I got into my room, it was freezing but I didn't touch anything because I didn't want to break something and make a bad impression to my new country. At 6 AM I took a shower, got dressed then waited in the hallway for my neighbors to come out so we could report our arrival. Sure enough, just before 7 AM they exited their room and we took the elevator down to the ground floor. I eagerly started walking towards the exit. One of them grabbed me by my left arm and pulled me in the opposite direction. Not wanting to piss them off and assuming they knew what they were doing, I followed them. We took some steps down, and then took a right turn and there was a huge room filled with rows of tables and chairs—a cafeteria. There was a line formed next to a row of food, and we got in line and I pointed at what I wanted to eat.

After breakfast I stopped by the front desk and offered to pay for my breakfast (I didn't want to come across as a freeloader). But the guy refused again. I scratched my head in thought, "I slept and ate in here, free of charge. I heard this country was rich, but this is ridiculous! I'm sure I'm missing something. Oh well, I'll find out later." The people that I was with were Iranians. After having breakfast all three of us headed towards the university on foot to report our arrival. From time to time I was looking back and taking mental pictures of the path so in case I lost my companions I could still get back to my hotel by myself. We arrived at Strong Hall, climbed some stairs and entered the Dean of Foreign Student's office to report our arrival. It was around 9 AM on August 24, 1971.

The secretary gave us some papers and the Iranians started filling them out page after page. The secretary would glance at us from time to time because I wasn't doing anything, just sitting there. The Iranians finished and they left. The secretary finally realized that I needed some help, walked into an adjacent office and a gentle black guy wearing glasses came out and motioned me to come into his office. I placed my passport and all the papers I had with me on his desk. He started filling out the paperwork for me. After he finished he motioned me to go. I returned to my hotel room, laid on my bed, put both hands under my head and stared at the ceiling. I felt overwhelmed.

"This is going to be much harder than I thought. How am I going to communicate and how am I going to keep the wheel turning?" A cloud of despair appeared on my horizon, but it only lasted for five minutes.

I said to myself, "I can't let obstacles appear bigger than me. I need to stare down at them from above. There is nothing I can't handle." I got my confidence back again and with that, I fell asleep.

Now, I am going to describe an out of body experience. At the outset I would like to say that I am skeptical about these experiences. Whether they really happen or are products of the brain under extreme duress, that I don't know. Personally, I have a clear and vivid recollection even after thirty-eight years and it went like this.

I hear a knock on my door. I am aware that I just arrived in America and that I don't know how to respond in English. I see my body laying on the bed and it looks more like it is dead than asleep. I hear a second knock.

"Come on," I am urging my body, "wake up somebody is at the door! I am a spirit, spirits can't talk but you can."

I woke up drenched in sweat and I couldn't breathe fast enough. Finally, I managed to say "embros", meaning "go ahead" in Greek. The door opened and a big guy with dark, curly hair walked in looking like a sumo wrestler. I felt vulnerable and was still trying to catch my breath from my out of body experience. I was trying to figure out if he is a friend or a foe from his demeanor.

Finally, he said, "Are you Pantelis Rahmanidis?"

"Yes," I said. Then he said something that I didn't understand. Next he said something half in English and half in Greek. My heart missed a beat.

"Are you Greek?" I asked.

"No man, I am a Cypriot."

"Oh hell," I said, "You speak my language and that's all that matters. How did you find me?"

"My name is Michael Economides. Alex, from Ethiopia, the guy who helped you with your paper work this morning— he is in my chemistry class and he ran into me at the Student Union eating lunch. He told me that a new guy from Greece just arrived; he didn't know where you were staying but that you badly needed help. So I checked the new arrivals in all the dormitories and I found you at Templin Hall."

"So, this is a dormitory? That's why they wouldn't take my money?"

"Yes," Michael said. "They assigned you a new room, number 214 and a roommate from Chicago."

"Michael, I need to transfer my money from Chase Manhattan to a local bank and buy shoes and clothes."

"Sure, but what happened to your toes?" They were bloody and looked awful. "What happened was I bought these shoes in a hurry to match my suit but they were at least one size smaller than my feet."

Later that day I moved into room 214 and met my roommate, Eric Beaver. He was just seventeen years old, a freshman. He was planning to major in Chemical Engineering. The next day I located where the Intensive English Center was and marked the shortest route to my dormitory. "Around this axis I will learn everything I need to know about America."

Chapter 7: Attending the Intensive English Center

The Intensive English Center had eight levels of language proficiency. I was attending the first level classes. The grading was A, B, C, D, F but the F was split into F1 and F2. F1 had three sub-grades and F2 had seven sub-grades, with Z at the bottom being the worst grade. My first grades were Z. It was tough, I couldn't understand a thing, those sounds were so strange that I always kept my dictionary with me. I would learn a word then I would go to the next and would forget the previous word. My brain was burning, nothing would stick for long! Each time I would look at a word and didn't recognize it, I would check my dictionary and place a red dot next to the word so I could keep track of how many times I looked at that word. One day in my dorm room a word looked familiar but I couldn't remember its meaning. I looked it up again and I saw a cluster of red dots next to it. I counted them up to thirteen! Out of frustration I hit my desk with my fist so hard I thought the desk cracked but it didn't. At that very moment I promised myself that I would learn the English language so well that the only way people would realize I am a foreigner would be because of my accent.

There were eight Greek students at University of Kansas and we would meet almost every weekend at somebody's house or apartment. I would learn a few words during the week then spend the weekends with the Greeks. By Monday, I could not remember a thing. I asked them to please speak English, as all of them could speak it very well, but they told me that I would not be able to understand them.

"Soooo," I said, "what do you care, I didn't come over here to perfect my Greek, I need my ears to practice the English sounds."

They replied with "Nope, we're proud to be Greeks and we'll speak our language."

"Fine," I told them, "I will not show up from now on." And so I forced myself into total isolation. The English language was like a wall blocking my path but I was determined to break it down and eventually travel through it.

Eric Beaver, my roommate, was a really nice guy. This was his first time away from home and I had nobody so we became very good friends. He would put a real effort into helping me with the language and teach me some things about America. I would say a few words and he could sometimes understand the whole sentence and other times I would say what I thought was a complete sentence but he would only understand a few words.

I remember him asking me: "Have you heard of Walter Cronkite?"

"No."

"Bob Hope?"

"No."

"Johnny Carson?"

"No."

"Billy Graham?"

"No."

I did not recognize any of these names, and he was amazed that I had not heard of them. Eric would often play a tape of Hubert Humphrey and George Garlin. He tried to explain to me the punch line about Hubert Humphrey by saying "short,

PAUL P RACHMANIDES

short, short" but I couldn't get it. Much later I realized that he was referring to his alter ego, telling him to stop talking. Also, he told me there are seven words you can't say on TV and he would pronounce all of them but I didn't understand a thing. Eric decided that I should practice. He asked me to pronounce a word.

I did it loudly and he said "Ssh, not too loud." It turned out to be the F word.

We would go to the cafeteria or to McDonalds for cheeseburgers together, and hang out a lot. I depended on him and I felt secure in America with him. At the Intensive English Center I was the only Greek. So, I was not able to talk to anyone. On breaks, I used to lean my back against the wall and observe everybody. There were three main groups: Spanish, Orientals and Iranians.

About a week before Thanksgiving our teacher said something that I didn't fully understand so I went over to him. Using my dictionary, he helped me understand that students who had no plans for Thanksgiving could spend Thanksgiving with an American family. For years, many American families had been signing up with the school's Administration department to host foreign students over short holidays like Thanksgiving. He went on to explain that if I wanted to sign up to stay with a family, I would have to do so in another room on campus. I didn't know where the room was, so he asked me if I knew where Strong Hall (the administration building) was. I said yes, and he drew me a map explaining how to get to the room from Strong Hall. I found the room near Strong Hall, where a black man was manning a table. He asked me something in English but I could not understand him. I motioned with my hands that I wanted to sign up.

He asked me where I was from and I replied "Greece."

Amazingly enough, he began speaking to me in Greek! He went on to explain that his father was a Greek who worked for a Greek construction company in Africa where he met his wife. His father taught this guy how to speak Greek as he was growing up. (I believe he was either from Congo or Kenya). I was flabbergasted—a non-Greek was speaking Greek to me, in America! This black guy went on to say that he would sign me up with a very good family who would contact me and arrange for everything. Two days before Thanksgiving a friend of Mark's (one of the family's sons) who was attending the University of Kansas picked me up along with a guy from Mexico. We were going south on a US interstate, in the heartland of America. I felt a sense of privilege and accomplishment. I felt very lucky and was grateful that my dream had come true.

We spent Thanksgiving with the Anderson family, who were very gracious to us. They had two sons: Tim age twenty and Mark age nineteen and one daughter: Jill age thirteen. Mrs. Anderson prepared some delicious dishes for Thanksgiving dinner. We prayed and gave thanks before every meal then watched TV and played ping-pong. I noticed the Mexican guy could communicate with them pretty well but I was communicating only with the motion of my hands. On Thanksgiving Day all of us gathered in the family room to watch football. The game was between Oklahoma and Nebraska. I didn't understand the game and didn't care to watch it but I had to be with everybody. At one point I saw a guy taking the ball at the twenty yard line run and cut this way and that, dodging everybody from the opposing team through the midfield and he ended up bursting into the end zone. After watching his spectacle, I became interested in learning about football. I insisted on learning his name and found out it was Johnny Rodgers.

The next day it was time to go back, but I wanted to express my gratitude to the Anderson family in English. I secretly wrote a short paragraph of thanks in Greek and with the help of my dictionary I translated it into English. I memorized it as quickly as I could. Mr. and Mrs. Anderson, the Mexican guy and I were standing outside saying goodbye when I started saying what I had memorized. Tears appeared at Mrs. Anderson's eyes. Mr. Anderson grabbed me with both arms from my waist and lifted me up. He was a short, fragile man and I was 6'3# weighing 195 lbs.

I became nervous, thinking, "Please put me down; I don't want you to fall backwards and ruin the moment." Fortunately, he did not fall over and we left in good spirits.

By the end of the fall semester 1971 I got a work permit from the Immigration and Naturalization Service. In January 1972 I started working in our dorm's cafeteria as a dishwasher. Mr. Steirus (not sure about the correct spelling) was the boss. He gave me the additional work of washing pots and pans. I liked it because I was learning more words. One day he asked me to follow him. He showed me a big barrel half full with water and a sack full of potatoes. He sat halfway on a stool, picked up a potato and peeled it. After peeling the potato he dropped it into the barrel. He did it again, then handed me the peeler and left. Well, I got the message. When I peeled all of the potatoes in the sack I returned to his office. The door was open and I saw him deep in thought over his papers. I just stood there thinking that he would notice me.

When he did I said "Finito!" while moving both of my hands for emphasis.

He looked at me a little bit puzzled, then got up and slowly approached the barrel. The barrel was full of peeled potatoes. He checked the empty sack and looking at me said something emphatically. I didn't know whether he was happy or not but I was itching to find out.

I asked my roommate to go down and ask Mr. Steirus what he said earlier. Eric walked back into our room with a smile from ear to ear.

"Pantelis, Mr. Steirus said "Daaamn, you are the fastest potato peeler I have ever seen."

Sensing that Mr. Steirus was happy with my performance, I approached him the next day for more work. From then on he would call me first and I never said no. There were days I was working seven to nine hours—from breakfast through dinner! That meant on those days I had to cut classes.

Working in the cafeteria, I realized I was making real progress with my English. I bought a couple Political Science books because I knew that eventually I would be majoring in Political Science. At first the words were bigger than my peripheral vision but I thought if I keep looking at them they will become smaller and smaller. Eventually, they did and by February of 1972 I realized I had developed a better system to learn the language than the Intensive English Center!

When I was not working, I would practice my eye to condense the words then learn their meaning. Eventually I was able to understand sentences. By doing so, the grammar, syntax and spelling were already imbedded into the sentence. From then on it was just a matter of accelerating the process. I also watched the news and movies on TV, this helped my ear get a good practice and conceptualize a story.

In the beginning I couldn't get much but as they say, "Practice makes perfect".

About two weeks before spring break in 1972 I received a letter from the Andersons stating that they would be delighted to have me back for spring break if I had no other plans. My roommate wrote back a letter saying I would be happy to return. Their son's friend picked me up and took me to El Dorado. Mr. Anderson was a band director and a music professor at the local college called the El Dorado Junior Community College. He gave me a tour of the college and we talked to Mr. Cummings, the Dean of Foreign Students. I asked him what grade in English I needed to score in order to attend this college.

He said "None, you can take whatever courses you want to and you can always drop the ones you can't keep up with. In addition, you can pre-enroll for the fall semester of 1972."

"Fantastic," I said, and so I pre-enrolled for seventeen credit hours, five of which were in French I. Now I was supposed to learn French in an English class where I am not sure my English will be any good, but I took it as a challenge.

Upon returning from spring break, I stopped attending all classes at the Intensive English Center. I was working a lot at the cafeteria and I intensified my learning system. In early May 1972 Mr. Steirus told me that he had to split my April check into two and mail the second half to El Dorado, Kansas at the end of May because I made much more money in one month than the University would allow any one student to make. He was obligated by the school to spread the work around to as many students as possible so no student could make more than $160 in any given month. I made $287 in April so Mr. Steirus wrote me a check on the spot for $160 and promised me that he would mail the balance to me, which he did.

I got a D from the Intensive English Center and moved to El Dorado, Kansas. The Andersons found a room for me to rent in an elderly lady's house who was a member of their church. They also helped me get a summer job; the owner of a factory was a member of their church too.

During the summer of 1972 I worked at a factory where we were making the styrofoam part of a helmet. Beads would fill up the mold, and then steam would fuse them together. Water would splash them for three minutes or so, then the mold would open and we would throw the finished product into an enclosed area and our clothes would get doused with water. Pay was $1.80 / hour working the graveyard shift from 11PM to 7 AM. After work I would take a shower, eat something and go to the college's library where it had a unique method of teaching English.

I sat in a booth and put on a headset. On a monitor in front of me the text was displayed and through the headset I could hear someone reading what was on the monitor in front of me. After hearing the text spoken I would practice writing it down then go to the next text. I did this every day until 1 or 2 PM, then I would eat lunch and hit the sack. I would wake up at 10 PM and was at work by 11 PM.

Even though I had my own place the Andersons would constantly invite me to their house. The whole family was very supportive of me, helping me with my English and teaching me by example. I was going with them to the Presbyterian church every Sunday and had dinner with them at their house after church. At times we would watch television or just visit with each other. The Anderson family helped me grow into the American culture and I was observing their every move.

My learning of the English language was very unstructured. Sometimes I would mispronounce a word or a phrase or I would misunderstand something. The Andersons would try very gently to correct either my pronunciation of a word, a phrase or would explain to me if I didn't understand something. I would like to mention three examples.

First, "At Avis we try harder."

I asked, "Mr. Anderson, why do they try harder?"

"Because they are #2 but they want to become #1."

Second, we were watching a nature show and at one point I said "That's a Hartford."

The Andersons looked a little confused and said, "Paul, that's a deer."

"No, no," I said. "The other day I saw this animal on TV and it was called the Hartford."

The Andersons said to me, "Paul, Hartford is the name of an insurance company and this animal is their mascot; deer is the name of the animal."

Third, one afternoon Mr. Anderson, their little daughter Jill and I were watching television. After a while Mr. Anderson said that in a few minutes he had to go do something.

Trying to show that I was learning new phrases I said, "You don't have to rush off, you faxes." But with my thick accent, it sounded more phonetically like "fuckxes"

Both Mr. Anderson and Jill looked at each other a bit startled then Mr. Anderson said, "Paul, what are you trying to say?"

"Well Mr. Anderson, the other day you had some friends of yours visiting here and when they got up to leave you said to them 'you don't have to rush off you fuckxes.'"

"Ohhh, I see…" Mr. Anderson said. "Paul, the word is folks; say **folks**."

A few days later I realized how what I said sounded and felt very embarrassed. "I am sorry for what I said the other day, Mr. Anderson."

"Don't worry about it Paul, we know you meant well."

I can mention countless other examples where the Andersons were shepherding me into the American language and culture. After a while I realized that they were treating me like one of the family. I no longer could call them Mr. and Mrs. Anderson.

So, one afternoon when we were watching television I waited for a commercial.

As soon as one came on I said, "Mr. and Mrs. Anderson, can I call you Mom and Dad?"

Both of them looked at each other and said, "Paul, if that's how you feel, we'll be very happy. We consider you our son." From then on until to this day they call me son and introduce me as their son. Tim, Mark and Jill call me 'big brother'. We keep in touch and at times we get together. Unfortunately, Dad passed away some time ago.

Chapter 8: My College Years

The beginning of the fall semester of 1972 found me as a freshman in an American junior college. I was somewhat tense and worried as to whether or not my English skills were good enough to keep up with my courses. During the first half of the first semester I was sitting straight up, my back never touched the back of my chair, focused on the lesson. I would constantly look at my teacher making sure I could hear and understand every word they were saying. Keeping up with all of my classes was of paramount importance to me. I was afraid if I missed a word or a sentence that it would snowball and I would fall behind. By mid semester I realized that I was doing well, that's when I started leaning back in my chair and relaxing in class. My first semester's GPA was 3.18 out of 4.00. The Dean of Foreign students Mr. Cummings called Mr. Anderson and said "You're not going to believe this but Paul's GPA is 3.18!"

In the fall semester of 1974 I was a junior at the University of Kansas transferring 63 credit hours, 16 of which were in French. I then took the TOFEL test and scored an A minus. I went back to Templin Hall and my new roommate was, again, from Chicago (the Kellingsworth suburb). I was doing well with my coursework. Someone mentioned to me that it would be a good idea to get a minor in Economics. Combining Political Science with Economics would give me a better perspective. I saw the point and eagerly started taking Economics classes.

In the summer of 1975 I went back home to Greece for the first time. My relatives came over to our house to greet me, including my Uncle Pete and his family all the way from Alexandroupolis.

At one point my mom approached me and with a low voice said to me, "Your Uncle Pete told me he is having a hard time convincing himself to do what he promised you he would do just before you left for America. What did he promise you?"

"Mom," I said, "Tell Uncle Pete not to worry about it. Ask him to tell you."

Most of my courses in my senior year were just Political Science and Economics. Sometimes I would come out of a Political Science class somewhat sad or mildly depressed. I could see how an inefficient political system was adversely affecting economic activity. The governmental sector would produce waste and inefficiencies but no one would be held responsible. Some governmental policies would come into direct conflict with market forces—the end result being inflation, stagnation, stagflation, recession and fears of possible depression on the way. Only when the policies were right would the economy grow.

On the other hand, in my Economics classes I would learn about planning, production and how to cut costs while increasing output to improve efficiency. Freedom of action, expansion, personal responsibility, rewards for success and punishment for failure were lessons taught in Economics. Three of my favorite fundamental principles are:

"There is no such thing as a free lunch"—Milton Friedman.

"The supply will always meet the demand."

"The system is the solution."—Ma Bell. I believe that if you violate these principles, the economy will pay a price.

The only Economics class that I didn't like was Public Finance. During the whole semester the course dealt with how to tax this and that and everything else. For example, I was working as a waiter about thirty hours a week at the best restaurant in town called The Eldridge House. I was making $2.25 per hour plus tips. I never knew for sure if I would make enough money to pay for my tuition and expenses for the next semester. You see, I was paying out of state tuition throughout my college years. The out of state tuition was three times as much as in state tuition. Tips would vary between 35 cents and 50 cents per customer during lunch to several dollars during dinner. And now the government wanted to tax my hard earned tips!!!

I came to the United States specifically to study Political Science and either teach or work for the Government, preferably in the Defense Department, both because of my military experience and my personal interest in Soviet affairs. By the time I got to graduate school I started cooling off to this idea and found myself gravitating towards the private sector. In December 1976 I graduated with a B.A. in Political Science with 21 hours in Economics. I didn't attend the graduation ceremonies as I had to work. I was taking graduate level courses in International and Comparative Politics in the spring and fall of 1977. By now I realized that my heart and mind belonged to the private sector, but how could I make the jump? I certainly couldn't go back and get a B.A. in Business. I was looking for a bridge to cross into the private sector.

In October of 1977, while drinking from a water fountain in the Political Science building, I noticed a bulletin board stuffed with many bulletins. A ceramic color looking one caught my eye. I strolled leisurely over to the bulletin board and started reading it.

It read: "Thunderbird, the American Graduate School of International Management." At first I thought it was an advertisement for the Air Force. Further down it stated that it was a private school offering business courses to people who wanted to have a career with a multinational corporation. It also stated that corporations actively recruit at the school. Upon graduation, a student would receive a Master's degree in International Management. The degree required 48 hours and a student can transfer only 6 graduate hours from another graduate program.

I said to myself: "This is too good to be true—this is the bridge that I was looking for but how come I never heard of it before? Is the school really any good?"

I noticed that Professor Clifford Ketzel posted the bulletin—that's my Political Science professor and advisor. I asked him about the school and he spoke highly of it. I thought that because he posted the bulletin he might be biased, so I decided to find an independent opinion.

I thought the Dean of the Business Department would give me an accurate assessment of the school, so the next morning I walked into the business department and his secretary said, "Do you have an appointment?"

"No mam, I don't."

"The Dean is very busy, you must make an appointment."

"Mam, It is urgent that I make a decision now and the Dean's opinion will greatly help me make the right one. I only have one question and he can answer it in thirty seconds or less. May I please talk to him."

She stared at me with a look that said, "You're a pushy one, aren't you." But she walked into the Dean's office anyway. Coming out she said, "The Dean will see you in a few minutes."

When he did, I greeted him and said "Dean, thank you for your time. What can you tell me about the Thunderbird School in Glendale, Arizona?"

He paused for a few seconds then said, "I will not put it on the same tier as the Ivy League schools but I would put it just below them. It is a very good school and I highly recommend it."

I was pleasantly surprised. "But Dean, how come I never heard of it?"

"You and the general public may not know about the school, but corporations do."

"Dean, you just helped me make up my mind. I am going to attend that school. Thank you very much."

I applied and was accepted. I transferred six graduate credits and entered the school in the summer of 1978 carrying twelve credit hours. In the spring of 1979 I had flybacks (where the corporation flies you to their headquarters and back) with Johnson & Johnson in Brunswick, New Jersey, Eli Lilly in Indianapolis and Foot, Cone & Belding in Chicago. I got no offers. In May of 1979 I graduated and faced the real possibility that I may not be able to stay and live in this country—the country I had fought so hard to get in and be assimilated into. But I wasn't about to give up. I moved into the house of a friend of mine without paying rent because I was practically broke. I went to the school's library and through Standard & Poor', I picked about forty-five companies and sent them my resume along with a cover letter. I kept a list of all the companies and the person's name my cover letter was addressed to.

Chapter 9: My Year with CBS

Owens-Corning Fiberglass flew me to Toledo, Ohio for an interview. They had a head office in Athens and were doing big business in Saudi Arabia. The idea of going back to Greece didn't sit very well with me but I said none of that to them. They made me an offer on the spot. I told them that I needed to think about it and would let them know. Within a day or two from getting back home my roommate left a note for me on the table.

It said: "Mr. de Rougemont called and said you need to call and talk to Paul Russell because Mr. de Rougemont is going out of the country."

Immediately, I started checking my list to find out which company Mr. de Rougemont worked for. Towards the end of the list I see:

CBS Records International
Peter de Rougemont
Senior Vice President
(N.Y. city address)

"Records, what kind of records are we talking about?" I wondered. "If it is financial I am not good at it and not interested but if it is music records that would be cool."

I dialed the number and a secretary connected me to Paul Russell. He told me "Paul, Mr. de Rougemont is our Senior Vice President who directs our Music Business in Europe. He is based in Paris, France. Twice a year he comes to New York City for meetings. He received your letter the day before he left for Europe. He asked me, along with my colleagues, to interview you here in New York and make a recommendation to him. So, when are you coming to New York?" I thought it was a very strange question. I was expecting him to say "We'll pay for your airfare and make hotel reservations."

"Mr. Russell, I am not planning on coming to New York anytime soon because I am broke." Silence. First five seconds, then ten, fifteen and twenty seconds passed. I knew from school that in negotiations he who breaks the silence loses. I held my breath.

Finally, he said "Paul, when we interview people we do not pay for their airfare, they come to us in New York and beg us for an interview. But if you agree to pay for your hotel, we'll pay for your airfare. I agreed and was told that in a couple of weeks they would let me know where I could pick up my ticket.

Indeed, two weeks later I flew to New York. I met Mr. Russell at about 10:30 AM and we talked for about forty-five minutes. Out of the many questions Mr. Russell asked me one still sticks out.

"Do you see a difference between the working environment of the United States and Europe?"

I answered: "Yes, Mr. Russell. Americans level with you and talk **to** you while the Europeans talk **at** you or down to you. Sometimes they even act as if they're doing you a favor by talking to you! I dislike that kind of attitude."

Then, he told me the Treasurer of the company along with the Director of Planning would take me to a French restaurant for lunch. Mr. Russell was a Vice President of Administration.

While we were walking, the two gentlemen were talking about an impending lay off. At one point the Treasurer asked the Director, "How many people are we talking about?"

"About 300," the Director replied. That felt like a chilly sprinkler on my face. What kind of a chance would I have to get hired if the company is on the brink of laying off about 300 people? But, perhaps that wouldn't have any impact on my chances.

We got back around 2 PM and Mr. Russell informed me that, "the Vice President of Finance would like to interview you tomorrow because he is very busy today. Plus, you need to talk to Ed Moore, the Director of Personnel."

I was pleased to hear that more people wanted to talk to me, that was a good sign, but I couldn't afford to pay my second hotel night. Sensing what made me worry Mr. Russell quickly added: "We will pay for your hotel, Paul, and my secretary will change your flight for tomorrow afternoon. We'll take care of everything and then he handed me a $50 bill.

"Petty cash," he said, and recommended that I have dinner at an Italian restaurant across the street. (This is how I learned what the phrase "petty cash" meant).

The next day, after being interviewed by the Vice President of Finance and Mr. Moore, Mr. Russell told me that, "We will compare notes and make a recommendation to Mr. de Rougemont. You will hear from us in about two weeks." With that, I flew back to Phoenix.

I felt excited and privileged, wondering how far this would go. I didn't want to shut this door prematurely by accepting the Owens-Corning offer, and so I decided to delay my response to them. Two weeks later I received a telegram asking me to call Mr. Moore.

When I did he asked me, "Paul, how does your schedule look like at the end of August?"

"It's wide open, Mr. Moore."

"Good, because we would like to fly you to Paris." My ears started buzzing. Certainly he didn't mean Paris, France!

I asked: "Mr. Moore, do you mean Paris as in Paris, France?"

"Yes Paul, that's the one!" I was in a state of shock. I never heard of anybody being flown overseas for an interview. Making every effort to keep cool I said, "That's great, Mr. Moore, thank you." On August 29, 1979 I flew from Phoenix, Arizona to Paris, France.

Mr. de Rougemont and Jacques Ferrari, Vice President of Business Development, took me out to lunch. Half an hour after we returned from lunch, Mr. de Rougemont handed me a one page paper and said, "Read it over and if you agree, kindly sign it." It was a job offer as an Executive Trainee to be assigned somewhere in Europe. I signed it partially because it did not mention Greece. I flew back to Phoenix, picked up my stuff and returned to Paris.

"You are Paul and I am Peter," Mr. de Rougemont told me. Within a few days I was sent to Brussels for four months. The highlight of my stay in Brussels was twofold. First, the group "Supertramp" performed in Antwerp and I met them back stage. Second, when I escorted the group "Chicago" from Brussels train station to the airport so they could fly to London. They were preparing for their world tour when they were stuck in Paris because of a strike so they took the train to Brussels. Peter Cetera, the group's lead singer, gave me a signed photo of the group.

After Brussels, I was sent to Nicosia, Cyprus for four months. The highlight was when CBS flew me to Israel to attend the Billy Joel concert in Jerusalem. In May of 1980 I was sent to Athens, Greece and promptly fell into a deep depression. I had come full circle!!! I felt I let myself down by taking my eyes off the prize. I had compromised my goal in life, which was to go to America, immerse myself into their culture, achieve success and stay there! It was the perfect job, but at the wrong place. I felt like a fish out of water and missed the States terribly. All the effort, sacrifice and risks that I had taken nine years earlier was for nothing. When I left Greece in 1971, I shut the door behind me. Becoming part of America was my goal, my purpose and my prize.

Fast forward to 2007 and 2008: *Dr. Wayne Dyer and Pastor Rick Warren spoke on TV about the Power of Intention and the Purpose Driven Life, respectively. "You're right!" I shouted on both occasions. "I am a living proof of this!"*

I tried to shake it off to no avail. What intensified my depression was this: The general manager Mr. Sol Robinowitz asked the sales manager to take me out to meet the major wholesalers.

When we got back Mr. Robinowitz asked me: "Paul, what is your impression?"

"Mr. Robinowitz, everybody had a different complaint to express but one complaint was mentioned by everyone. The company does not take back warped records."

"Paul, did the sound come out good?"

"Yes Mr. Robinowitz but the needle was riding a rollercoaster. In the US those records would be returned, no questions asked."

"Paul, we're not in the US. If we were to take back warped records we would have to take back more than half of our product. The reason they are warped is that there is only one pressing plant in Greece and all the labels are pressing their records there. The plant, in order to meet the deadlines, does not allow enough cooling time."

"Mr. Robinowitz, how about walking into their offices and demanding more cooling time?"

"If we were to demand more cooling time they would refuse to do business with us. They have more demand than they can handle."

"Ok then, how about our plant in Holland supplies us with a good product."

"The Greek Government requires us to deposit the money in our bank six months in advance. We don't know the demand six months down the road plus that ties down our capital unnecessarily."

"Ugh," I thought. "Nothing's changed, I can't deal with this kind of bureaucratic nonsense. I need to get the hell out of here." From then on I was looking for the right moment.

After a week in Athens, I was sent to Thessaloniki to manage our subsidiary there. Talk about coming full circle!! I stayed in Thessaloniki in June, July and August of 1980.

The wholesalers in Thessaloniki had a different problem with the company. A past sales manager asked them to accept a larger delivery of records than they ordered for an upcoming concert and promised that the company would take back what was left over. Now the wholesalers were stuck with a dead product because the company refused to take them back as promised.

"No problem," I said. "I'll call Athens."

I called and was told the manager wasn't with the company anymore. I stated that it didn't matter if the manager was there or not now, the company needed to take the excess product back as promised.

They brushed me off saying "he shouldn't have made that promise." That was the straw that broke the camel's back. I sat down and wrote my resignation letter.

One might wonder why I accepted the job, knowing that I might end up in Greece. Well, CBS treated me extremely well. The sirens of the music world had an enormous pull on me—it looked to me like an exciting new frontier that would present challenges. Challenge brings out the best in me.

The highlight of my stay in Thessaloniki was in summer when Julio Inglesias came to town for a concert and I had a chance to meet him and take him to a restaurant by the beach.

In mid-June I met an older, well-educated, sharp Greek American lady named Leah Vlami who emigrated some years ago from Sacramento, California. She had her own falling out with her family. Christine, the daughter of her friend Dorothy (or Doti for short) from New Jersey was visiting her that summer and we hung out together. One day while I was visiting Leah in her condo her neighbor's young daughter came in with a long face saying she was depressed because things didn't go her way. Trying to cheer her up and show her that some people were going through more difficult times in their lives I started telling her what I went through to get my VISA. Midway through I sensed that she was getting bored and to check if she was paying attention I abruptly stopped talking.

At that very moment Leah emphatically said, "Paul, I command you to continue."

That irked me but being at her place I put a frozen grin on my face and said "Leah, what's with you?"

"Oh honey," she said, "you're not going to believe what I am about to tell you. But first I want you to finish. Please, go on."

I wrapped it up pretty quick then turned towards Leah and said, "Well Leah, what are you about to tell me?"

"Paul, our paths have crossed in the past." She couldn't be serious, I thought, I just recently met her.

"Paul," Leah continued, "I knew Mr. & Mrs. Peters. I've been to their place many times and Mrs. Peters came over to my place. As a matter of fact a bunch of us ladies got together and we would be meeting in our homes by rotation. Right after August 15, 1971 (August 15th is a major religious holiday in Greece, celebrating Mary, the mother of Jesus) we happened to be gathered at the Peters' home. In the past when Mr. Peters would come in from work he would look tired and withdrawn. He would say hi and make small talk for about a minute then would walk into his study. This time when he walked in he looked different. We noticed that he looked rested, happy and calm with a smirk on his face."

"His wife asked him, "Honey, what's that smirk on your face, did something happen today at the office?" Mr. Peters, still standing up, ran the fingers of both hands through his blonde hair and said, "Uhh yeah, today I granted a student VISA to a former hippy."

We were all holding our breath, waiting to hear what he would say next, but he said nothing. His wife said "Aaaaand?"

Mr. Peters replied, "Nothing, that's it." and walked into his study. We looked at each other not knowing what to make of it and went back to our girl talk. But that scene stuck in my mind. Paul, I bet he was talking about you!"

"Well Leah, what a small world. The dates sure match."

Christina returned to New Jersey in early August. August 31, 1980 was my last day at CBS. Leah gave me something for Christina and for her mother Dorothy, hoping I might rekindle my relationship with Christina. I liked her as a good friend but had no physical attraction towards her and I didn't want to force my emotions. And so, carrying Leah's gifts I was supposed to spend several days with them in New Jersey.

Chapter 10: My Second Coming

On Thursday, September 4, 1980 I arrived at the JFK airport in New York. The INS officer told me that I had to return to Greece because my tourist visa required a return ticket and mine was one-way. I told him I lived in the US for 8 years and went to college, so I could always buy a return ticket later. He told me that either I go back or I discuss my case with a judge on Monday.

I told him "I'll talk to the judge" and I crossed the checkpoint. He told me, "You are now under INS detention until you appear before an immigration judge on Monday."

I couldn't believe it. The country that I loved and fought so hard to be a part of is treating me like a common criminal. For the first time the issue of legality hit me in the face and I felt its impact. I realized that regardless of how I feel about America, if I was not a US citizen then in the eyes of the law I was just another foreigner. Up to that point the need never arose, but now it was clear and urgent: the only way for me to become a US citizen was to marry one. Her name was Doris ("Sandy") Bilbrey.

I met Sandy at the Point, a watering hole by the Camelback Mountains while attending Thunderbird school. She was a young, slim, sweet and gentle girl working as a secretary at Honeywell. I could have married her while in school but I had to take one more step before I could settle down and raise a family. I wanted to get a job and be secure and happy with it.

We kept in touch while in Europe and she was urging me to come back telling me how much she missed me.

At the airport, INS officers searched my suitcase and found nothing. Then, with their permission I called Dorothy, telling her what happened and that I didn't know where they were going to take me.

"Don't worry," she said, "We'll track you down."

One INS officer said to the other, "We're short on guards."

The other replied with. "We'll assign one on him, he's pretty big and he can handle him. Besides, in a few hours the other two guards will start their shift." My guard and I arrived at a Hotel near the airport and checked into a room on the 3rd floor.

At 7 AM sharp the next morning (Friday) two young guards came in and the first one left. The two new guards were friendly with me and I taught them how to play Backgammon. We talked and I told them a little bit about how I came to America and explained very briefly what I went through. They felt sorry for me, both saying that they couldn't believe the way the INS was treating me.

"Neither do I," I replied.

They went on: "You, Paul, are very calm. You don't give us any trouble like other people did. Those people tried to escape by jumping through the window."

I smiled and said, "Don't worry guys, I am not going anywhere, I am going to see the judge on Monday."

One of the guards said to the other, "What would happen to us if Paul escapes?"

"We would probably lose our jobs," the other one replied, "but don't worry we could find another one."

At noon we had lunch downstairs with the guards on either side of me. "We hate to do this to you, Paul" they said, "but we have to."

"No problem guys, I understand." Back in our room after lunch, one guard suggested we go out by the swimming pool.

Within seconds of him saying this, the room's telephone rang and the guard answered. Within a few seconds he started saying "Yes sir, no sir, yes sir" and after hanging up he walked away from the phone like a cheetah steps away in the presence of a lion, all the while he was looking at us and with his lips he mouthed, "This room is bugged." From then on we were careful what and how we said things. In the meantime the guards informed me that if the judge turned me down, the US Government would pay for my return ticket but that would mean deportation and I would never again be allowed into the US.

That freaked me out. For a couple hours I was really depressed. In the late afternoon the phone rang, and the guard who answered it said, "It is for you, Paul."

It was Dorothy! Speaking in Greek, I asked Dorothy if she could buy me a return airfare to Greece, promising her that I would pay her back upon my return.

She said, "No problem, we can buy it tomorrow and bring it to you on Sunday late afternoon or evening."

"That's fine Dorothy, but listen carefully. If you and Christina arrive at the hotel before 6:50 PM come up to our room. Any time after that, please, *please* stay in the Lobby and one of my day guards will pick it up."

"I got it," she said. The day guards and I quietly developed a plan in case the ladies arrived late. One of the guards would leave his jacket in the closet. He would find Dorothy and Christine downstairs and bring the ticket up to my room under the guise of getting his jacket. He would leave the ticket in the pocket of my jacket for me.

On Saturday afternoon my day guards said to me, "Get your jacket, we are going out."

I replied, "But we aren't supposed to leave the room!" and they told me, "Don't worry, you are with us." We got to the parking lot and into a car. We took the freeway for about twenty minutes and walked into an enclosed shopping mall.

"We want some fast food" they said and we got in line.

One of them said "Paul, do you see that newspaper stand? Will you go and get us a newspaper? Here is fifty cents." I walked over and picked up the paper and started walking back towards them. I noticed they were talking to each other with their backs towards me! I felt good that they trusted me enough to not keep an eye on me.

On Sunday, 7 o'clock arrived and the ladies had still not shown up but the night guards arrived and the day guards left. About 7:30 PM there was a knock on my room door.

"Who is it?" the inside guards asked. The day guard outside gave his name.

"What do you want?"

With an agitated voice the guard outside said, "I forgot my jacket, open up man."

The night guard was clearly bothered but walked over and opened the door. He let the day guard in then went back to watching television. The day guard closed the door (which was covering the closet), reached into the closet and picked up his jacket, then looked at me with a look that said the airplane ticket was in my jacket. I smiled at him thankfully. I never saw those two guys again, but I hope someday I run into them; I owe them a favor. Half an hour later I walked over to the closet and saw that the airplane ticket was indeed in my jacket.

The next day, early Monday morning, we arrived at the courthouse. A refined looking black man with sandy hair and wearing glasses approached me and said, "I am a public defender and I have been assigned to your case. There are many cases ahead of us but sit tight until I come back."

"Sir," I said, "I have a return ticket back to Greece."

Startled, he said, "Do you have it with you?"

"Let me show it to the prosecutor and see what she will say." My public defender returned about forty five minutes later and said to me, "The prosecutor agreed to drop the charge and the judge agreed."

Then I asked him, "Did the prosecutor say anything else?"

He told me, "She walked away shaking her head saying: 'That's impossible, that's impossible he was under guard 24/7."

At that moment two INS officers said to me, "Let's go for a walk." I thought that sounded weird but can you argue with them? While walking we arrived at a plane where people were boarding. They handed me my Greek passport but the top right corner was cut.

They said, "Go ahead and get on the plane."

"I need to pick up my stuff from the hotel," I told them.

"Don't worry, your suitcase will arrive at the Athens airport tomorrow afternoon."

Indeed, it did arrive but in bad shape. From Athens I flew to Alexandroupolis where my Uncle Pete was an employee of the State Government for more than 20 years. I needed a new passport and went to my Uncle Pete for help. He approached the man in charge of new passports and confidentially said, "I suspect that my nephew works for the US Government, I think the CIA. He needs a new passport now, he lost the old one, don't ask too many questions but can you help?"

"You know I could get into trouble but, I'll go ahead and issue one."

"Thank you, I owe you one," my Uncle Pete said.

An hour later my Uncle Pete was coming down the long stair case looking like Moses carrying the 10 Commandments. With a smile indicating accomplishment, he handed me my brand new passport.

"Uncle Pete, you're the greatest, thank you."

I went to Thessaloniki and got a new tourist VISA and purchased a round trip to the US. On September 17, 1980 I arrived again at the JFK airport. An INS officer gave me a 30 day VISA. I arrived at Dorothy and Christine's house in New Jersey and paid them back. They had a small grocery store on the ground floor and they were living upstairs. The store downstairs also sold books, and I bought and read "The Camera Never Blinks" by Dan Rather. I have been a fan of Dan Rather partly because parts of our lives were parallel and partly because he was one hell of a reporter. I closely followed his battles with the Nixon administration and his becoming a bright star of CBS News. I understand he also wrote "The Palace Guards."

A week later I left Dorothy and Christine's place and flew to Phoenix. Sandy and her twin sister Debbie picked me up from the airport and I moved in with them. I wanted to find out if Sandy was still seriously interested in me now that I didn't have a job. I took my time and applied for a VISA extension from the Phoenix INS office.

In early November of 1980 Sandy asked me, "Do you want to get married?"

We got married on November 15, 1980 in Las Vegas. That is when my 20 year Odyssey began. Either in January or February the Phoenix INS interviewed us for my Green Card. I believe the Green Card arrived in May of that year. To celebrate, we decided to take a vacation in San Diego sometime in early June.

Chapter 11: My 20 Year Odyssey

Earlier in the year I sent a bunch of resumes to companies and to several executive search firms. Just before we left for San Diego I received a phone call from Harold Frank, a headhunter with Search Masters in New Port Beach, California. He said the person my letter was addressed to no longer worked for the firm; but he looked at my resume and would like to interview me. He asked when I could come to New Port and I told him about our pending trip to San Diego. I made an appointment for 11 AM on either a Thursday or Friday. He told me he taught Public Administration at Ivy League Schools.

He asked me many questions like, "What do you want to do with your life? Where do you see yourself in 5, 10, 20 years from now and how do you plan on getting there?"

At one point he asked me, "Paul, can you name a few millionaires?"

"Sure, Rockefeller, Ross Perot, Ford."

"No no no Paul, these guys are zillionaires. I am talking about 1-3 million net worth. I thought and I couldn't name one."

"I don't know any, Mr. Frank."

"Precisely," he said, "they are inconspicuous. They are all around us yet we cannot tell who they are. They don't wear fancy clothes and they almost never buy brand new cars. They drive good cars but used ones. They work for value, build equity and their bank account is very healthy. Who are they? Well, when you go back to Phoenix look around your neighborhood.

If you see a successful small business owner he is most likely a millionaire."

Wow, up to that moment I thought small business owners were small potatoes. Successful was the word Mr. Frank emphasized.

"But to open a business requires capital, Mr. Frank, and I don't have any of that."

"Paul, do you know how 80% of America's millionaires made their money?"

"No sir."

"They made it in real estate. They bought low and sold high. You only need a pencil and paper and I'm sure you won't have any trouble getting your Real Estate License. You can work for a real estate firm and make enough money from commissions to accumulate capital for your business."

That made sense, but it also looked like a tall order to me. I liked the idea of independence—not just financial but mental as well, where you are your own boss. But freedom is not free, it comes with strings attached like risk of failure, shortages and unpredictability until you reach that magic point called "Success". Overcoming overwhelming odds almost non-stop for the past nine years took a toll on me. I felt exhausted. I was looking for the security of a corporation with the predictability of a regular paycheck and the safety net of medical coverage or investment participation. The problem was those opportunities were available to me overseas but I was not interested anymore in an overseas assignment. So, for the time being I put this promising career path of becoming a small business owner on the back burner.

To keep up with household expenses while I was looking for a corporate job I got a temporary one at Wigwam as a waiter. Wigwam is a resort about 20 miles west of Phoenix near the town of Goodyear. The money was good but I also suffered the ultimate humiliation. One night some Thunderbird students and several faculty members came over for dinner and I was assigned to be their waiter.

The finance professor recognized me and with a facial expression of surprise and bewilderment said to me, "What are you doing here?"

I told him, "Professor Mills, it is a long story."

In early January of 1982 I got in touch with Jay Brandon III, my roommate at Thunderbird who was working for Texas Instruments in Houston, Texas.

"Come on down," he said, "Houston is bustling with activity and you can stay in my house while you look for a job."

Indeed, I drove to Houston in late January and got a job with Radio Shack as a salesperson. On March 15, Sandy and I arrived in Houston, Texas. By fall of that year it became apparent that Radio Shack was not for me, so I became a business broker. I had some success with that but nothing significant career wise. Sandy told me many times that she met the man who would become very rich. She was big on astrology with all kinds of charts and predictions. I thanked her for the encouragement but I didn't pay any attention to it.

Apparently, Sandy couldn't wait much longer for me to get rich so, in mid-August she asked me for a divorce. We split amicably and on August 23, 1983 she flew back to California. Her salary was a safety net and now it was gone. By now it became clear that Corporate America was not in the cards for me. With no safety net, I depended on commissions 100%—talk about pressure!

Now was the time to take Mr. Frank's advice to heart. I was aware of the overwhelming risks and the unpredictability but I wanted to become a successful small business owner. Striving to become a successful small business owner is like swimming with the sharks—you operate in a hostile environment because 80-90% of small businesses go belly up the first year. But this scary environment looked familiar to me. My military experience taught me how to jump behind enemy lines carrying very little and elude capture. I knew how to plan, organize, train and execute devastating raids against the enemy. "I've got nothing to fear but fear itself" to borrow President Roosevelt's famous line.

In early 1984, I got my real estate license and jumped head first into it. Residential sales were spotty and it didn't provide enough to cover my bills. To manage, I worked at night as a bartender at the River Oaks country club. While there I became friends with Joe Martino, a Vice-Officer with the Houston Police department working as security. Pursuing commercial real estate deals, I felt I would have a better chance to put money aside. In 1986 the price of a barrel of oil hit $11. Out of business signs were everywhere and there were a record number of bankruptcies. People were leaving Houston in droves. The Houston economy stalled in 1982 and was sliding downward, hitting bottom in 1986 and 1987. My survival became much more difficult but I was not about to go anywhere. In Houston, I felt at home from the very beginning and decided to weather the storm.

Weathering a storm means you have to take chances. In pursuing commercial real estate deals I felt I was rubbing shoulders with shady characters, possibly mob connected.

So, I asked my friend Joe Martino, "Joe, how can I make sure I don't fall into their orbit?"

He replied, "Paul, their money is good but don't ever let them do you a favor, you'll never be able to do enough to repay them." I pictured this advice as a safety suit just like a firefighter walking into a burning building expecting his suit to protect him.

I met John Kirkpatrick in 1982 when both of us were business brokers at Mylid, Inc. A very pleasant fellow, very easy going. By 1983 he no longer was a business broker and instead he hooked up with a group of Orientals who owned a number of businesses including restaurants. He introduced me to them as a good friend of his and a guy who might be of help with their real estate needs. The top guy of the group had the unusual nickname "Yellowbird." At times I would hang out with them but always on the periphery. One day one of them asked me for a favor. Would I be interested in finding a house for rent for a good friend of theirs who is moving to Houston from Los Angeles—but put my name on the lease. They of course would pay the rent money plus $125 a month for me. I felt a bit uneasy about it, but hoping this might lead to a big future commercial deal I accepted. What could go wrong with a house in the middle of a neighborhood?

A couple of months passed when one day the phone in my office rang. I picked up and heard a man's voice saying, "This is officer so-and-so with the Houston Police Department's Criminal Division. I need to talk to you and I would like to know when can we meet?"

I was stunned. What does the Criminal Division have to do with me? I needed to find out asap. "Sir," I said, "There is a Champ's Restaurant next to my office. I can be there in one minute. How soon can you get there?"

"In about ten minutes," he said. I could tell he was happy for agreeing to meet with him right away.

We sat at a table and he said, "I am going to show you a few driver's licenses and ask you to point out the person you rented the house to plus a few more questions. The FBI is ready to run all over you, but I can keep them at bay if you answer my questions truthfully. Looking at the driver's licenses, I pointed out the man I rented the house to.

The officer told me, "We think this person is the triggerman that killed an Oriental newspaper reporter in Los Angeles. Plus, he briefly turned the house into a high class prostitution place."

Visibly shaken and with a somewhat angry voice I said, "If I can get my hands on him, I'll kill him."

"No need for that" said the officer. "How much did they pay you for renting the house?"

"$125 a month, sir."

"I am happy with your answers and as far as I am concerned this will be it."

Adult Entertainment business was all the rage in the 80's. They were making money hand over fist. Caligula XXI was featured as the number one topless club in the nation by Playboy magazine in 1983. The co-owner was a Greek and the other was a German. I became friends with them hoping and urging them to let me find a second location. In the mid-80s I got to know the owners of the top 3 clubs: Dallas of Rick's cabaret and Mr. Luis Warren of Déjà Vu.

In late 1983 I talked to the owner of a restaurant called The Back Porch who also owned the land in a great location (on Highway 6, just north of Westheimer). He agreed to sell land and the building for 1.3 million. I approached Mr. Luis Warren and he got excited about it. A contract was signed by both the buyer & seller. My commission was set at $16,000—not enough to open a business but it was a start.

Just before closing Mr. Warren informed me that Dallas of Rick's Cabaret threatened to burn the place down if Luis went ahead with the deal, so he decided to back out, telling me, "I don't want to go to war with Dallas over this location."

Dallas tried to get it himself and when he failed he decided if he couldn't get it then no one else would.

I felt defeated and dispirited, but I tied my belt, dusted off my boots and said "On with the next deal!"

I realized that Dallas was an important person and someone I could do business with, so I approached him. From time to time he would call me and would tell me where I can meet him then, we would ride in a limousine looking at possible locations. On one of these rides we were on Westheimer going west and just passed Post Oak Boulevard when Dallas points to a 6 story office building and says: "I can take the whole top floor. It looks like more than half is empty. Check out with the owners if they would go for it."

I said, "Dallas there is no way they'll go for it. If this was a free standing building, then yes, we would have a good chance but an office building in the Galleria? It will never happen."

"Yeah, I guess you're right" said Dallas. After one of these rides he took me to his house and introduced me to his partner Robert who was a lawyer, saying this is Paul and he is helping us find a new location. A little bit later I called Dallas and told him that there is a good spot for sale on the feeder road of Highway 59 just south of Hillcroft. He said he would check it out with his partner Robert and get back to me. When I talked to him later that afternoon he said that Robert knew about it and he is already negotiating with them. I found it odd that he didn't know about it earlier in the day. At any rate, they bought the land & building and it became the Colorado Bar & Grill.

In the meantime I made small sales here and there. I kept getting credit card offers but I used them only when necessary and making only the minimum payments.

In late 1985 I was in a dire situation, financially speaking.

Someone approached me and asked, "Would you be interested in getting a sexually oriented permit in your name for a modeling studio? We will run the place and pay you well."

"No thanks, that's illegal and I don't want to get in trouble with the law."

"No no no," the guy said, "It is perfectly legal—the Vice Division of the Police Department issues the permit."

"Are you kidding me? If that's indeed the case I'll do it, what's more legal than when the police give their blessings." I did get the permit but I didn't feel comfortable because they never let me take a look inside, they always came up with excuses on why I couldn't get inside. Five months later I took my name off the permit. In August of 1986 I went back home to Greece for three weeks.

The next deal was an 8 story office building in an effluent area (1800 Augusta); I took the deal to Mr. Ternier. He wrote a 4.2 million with a 20% down payment. My commission was set at 1.5%. I was told that another group made a 3.5 million cash offer and bought the building. That was like a dagger through my chest.

Next was a 12.9 million deal. It was a marina called the Legend Point with condos on one side and plans to develop the other. The Horn Real Estate Company, one of the best, had the listing. I brought in the buyer. We worked on it for five months. The contract called for 12.9 million cash and my commission was set at $250,000. Finally, I could do something with that kind of money! The title company was Stuart Title in the Galleria, and on the day of closing the buyer never showed up.

"That's it!" I said, "I hate real estate—I need to get the hell out of this!"

In 1989 I approached a restaurant owner and asked him if he would be interested in converting his restaurant into a topless club.

"Sure," he said, "If I'll be a part of it." I found an investor and brought into the deal Harry, the former co-owner of Caligula XXI. The investor got 64% and the three of us split the remaining 36% 12% each. Finally, I own equity in an industry that's making good money. This time I am confident I'll make the money I need. We did all the remodeling ourselves and opened for business on March 15, 1990. Parisienne was the name of the club, on Gulf Freeway just south of Almeda Mall. Initially the place did well but soon after the investor started interfering. Something was happening under my nose but I couldn't prove anything. I grew frustrated. I could run the place like a business but the partners wouldn't let me.

A regular customer approached me one evening by the bar and said, "Paul, you don't belong here—you are out of place. You project yourself as a classy person, but here you are like a fly in a glass of milk. Go and do something else."

I was growing frustrated as the time went on. I realized that if you don't have the money you dance to someone else's music.

At the end of the shift on Halloween night I approached the investor and told him: "I am walking away from the place at this moment."

A guy from Palestine named Zouhair ("Mark") Adi used to come to the club and we became friends. At one point he told me that he was thinking about buying a gas station in Deer Park very cheap because the previous owner ran it into the ground. If I would agree to help him out and bring it back to life and make it a success then he would put up the money and we would go 50-50 on a second location. In late 1990 we took over the station. We cleaned it up, painted it and did minor remodeling. Within a few months we brought it back to life and it was doing pretty well. The station was across the street of the San Janito College. The college was offering classes for Truck Drivers because twice a week I was seeing students practice on 18-wheelers.

From time to time looking at them practice I said to myself, "I hope I don't fall to a level that I would have to become a truck driver." I had the impression that it was hard, lowly, dirty and dangerous work. Not to mention that I thought the pay was worth peanuts.

After a while I realized my friend had no intention on keeping his end of the bargain so I was looking for a way out. In early 1992 I went back to Greece for my brother's wedding. There I noticed a Greek brewery was licensed to make Russian Vodka. I knew that Vodka was the #1 liquor consumed in the US. I thought if I could just capture a small sliver of the market I would be doing great. I checked with Spec's, a major wholesaler, and they agreed to carry it if I would import. I borrowed about $25,000 from my dad and I went after it. In early 1994 a container full of Potemkin Vodka arrived in Houston, Texas. It moved pretty well in the first few months then it went dead. I sold the rest of it below cost just to get rid of it. I was out of breath, exhausted and I wished that if I could just close my eyes all this would go away like a bad dream.

"What's wrong with me?" I wondered. "I know I am not dumb, why can't I figure out something that would work for me?" The years were passing by and I had nothing to show as accomplishment.

The constant grind to survive year after year starved my mind of intellectual stimulation. My mind was stuck in intellectual steppes. Thank God in the early 90s I accidentally stumbled into and became a subscriber of Inc., Success and Discover magazines. I couldn't wait for the next issues to arrive and I would eagerly read each one of them cover to cover. From Inc., magazine I got a real education as to what I needed to do to run a successful small business. Inc., dealt with issues affecting small to medium-sized companies. One of my first recollections was an article about Mr. Stack of Springfield Remanufacturing Company in Springfield, Missouri. His open book management style helped make his company a success. Norm Brodsky helped me greatly with his practical advice on what to keep your eyes on and what pitfalls to avoid. In the mid-90s Inc. magazine featured an article about entrepreneurship written by a Harvard business school professor.

He defined entrepreneurship as the "relentless pursuit of an opportunity regardless of the resources on hand."

I shook up! This resonated with me—it was what I had been doing all my life—I was an entrepreneur at heart without even knowing! It was a Eureka moment for me.

At Thunderbird business school, there was no mention on entrepreneurship—emphasis was exclusively on large corporations and "big business". Inc. and Success magazines shed light that only an entrepreneur could be a successful small business owner.

At Success, Clement Stone was writing an essay on the back of every issue. At a particular issue the title stated: "You Failed? That's Terrific". I thought he was nuts. I said, he better present a convincing argument if he ever wants me to read his essays again. The point was, as long as you make a mistake for the first time that's OK—if you learn from it, you won't repeat it. Also, failing at something does not make you a failure, as long as you get up, dust off your boots, tighten your belt, lick your wounds and go at it again. There is success in failure and failure in success. What's really important is what you choose to pick from the experience.

"Successful people", Mr. Stone stated, "fail on average four times, before they hit it right."

"Well", I thought, "I have already failed more than four times, so now I am due for success, but in what?"

I had no money but I knew that he who has the gold makes the rules. So, I decided to come up with my own money first, then figure out what to do with it. I thought putting $50,000 in the bank would be enough.

Reading Discover magazine helped me escape the confines of planet Earth and the solar system. It also spurred me to energetically chase T.V. documentaries that dealt with cutting edge issues in theoretical physics, space and the Universe in general. To this day I still subscribe to Inc., and Discover magazines.

My mind dealt with cutting edge issues in theoretical physics such as the Big Bang (Georges Le'Maitre, George Gamow, Ralph Alpher and Robert Hermann).

SuperGravity (Michael Duff and the 11 dimensions).

SuperSymmetry "SuSy" (Gordon Kane and James Gates).

Cosmic Inflation (Alan Guth).

Cosmic background Radiation (Arno Penzias and Robert Wilson).

Steady State (Einstein, Fred Hoyle), Element formation (Fred Hoyle).

Supermassive black holes. The Nuker Team and Vera Rubin found a strong correlation between the mass of the supermassive black hole and the speed at which stars at the outer edge of the galaxy are moving, suggesting that the two might be connected at birth. In other words, supermassive black holes may have been instrumental in the creation of galaxies.

The visible Universe, Dark Matter, Dark Energy (Sean Carroll, Vera Rubin).

String theory (Michael Green, John Schwarz, Ed Witten, Brian Greene and James Gates).

Expansion of the Universe at an accelerating rate (Saul Perlmutter).

M Theory (Branes) Burt Orvut, Paul Steinhardt and Neil Turok.

The number 137 which relates to nature, the Fine Structure Constant.

I came to familiarize myself with names like Michael Faraday, Lavoisier, Newton, Maxwell, J.J. Thomson, Robert Brown and Brownian Motion, Ludwig Boltzman, Einstein (E=MC squared, Special and General relativity and Theory of Everything) and Ernest Rutherford.

Neils Bohr (Quantum Mechanics and the Quantum Jump), Werner Heisenberg and the uncertainty principle which states that, "Nature, at its most fundamental level is governed by chance and probability".

Other names and concepts I learned included James Cronin and Val Fitch and Charge Parity Violation, Wolfgang Pauli and the exclusion principle. Max Born and Pascual Jordan who developed most of the math to Heisenberg's Matrix mechanics on which "The Copenhagen Interpretation" was accepted at the Solvay Conference of 1927. Erwin Schrodinger (wave mechanics and wave function). Max Planck, the Planck particle and the "Planck Scale" of length, time and mass as well as the Planck Constant. Paul Dirac (antiparticles and mathematical beauty).

Alexander Friedmann and the Friedmann equation (8 pi G / 3)P = H squared + K. (That is the Greek letter rho, not P). According to Sean Carroll this is the most important equation in cosmology because it describes the curvature of space. Edwin Hubble (the red shift and the Hubble constant). James Chadwick, Lisa Meitner, Wolfgang Pauli, Ray Davis, John Bahcall and the elusive neutrino. Richard Feynman (QED, Path Integral Formulation, Superfluidity of supercooled liquid helium, Feynman diagrams, the Feynman lectures on Physics, pioneering the field of quantum computing and introducing the concept of nanotechnology.

Murray Gell-Mann (Quark Model).

Stephen Hawking (black holes, Hawking Paradox, Hawking radiation and Theory of Everything). Micho Kaku "Time" series and parallel worlds. Neil de Grasse Tyson (My Favorite Universe). Brian Greene (The Elegant Universe, The Fabric of the Cosmos). Jim Al-Khalili (Atom: Key to the Cosmos, Clash of Titans and the Illusion of Reality). Lisa Randall and many others.

My father, sensing my suffering again renewed the invitation and urged me to give up everything and go back. "All of us will help you do something over here" he said.

From time to time my father would call and ask me "Did you buy a house?"

"No Dad, I didn't."

"Did you get married?"

"No Dad, I didn't." It was implied that if I wasn't married and didn't own a house then all this effort was for nothing.

He would ask me how long would I "keep trying to be a success?"

At one point I said: "Dad, if one has to ask how long, maybe he hasn't waited long enough. As long as it takes Dad, as long as it takes."

The easy thing for me to do was to go back. But doing so would indicate that I failed in America, a place where "the streets are covered with gold and all one has to do is pick it up" and I couldn't even do that. That thought gave me the creeps, and I decided to never accept that for as long as I breathed.

In 1997 I really hit bottom. Seventeen years after Thunderbird I was broke, over $25,000 in credit card debt and had no health insurance. The constant pressure to survive was wearing me out, but I never complained. During the dark days between the two interviews with Consul Peters back in the summer of 1971, I promised myself that if I managed to set foot in America I would never complain about anything, no matter how tough things might get. To this day I have kept my promise. Looking back, I am thankful to John Peters for denying me a VISA the first time. That ravved up my determination and willingness to suffer and to sacrifice to…. NO LIMIT. My desire to come over here and to succeed was so intense, I believe, it could have matched the intensity of a gamma ray burst. From time to time, when things were really tough, I used to stand in front of a mirror, slightly raise both my shoulders, crack a shy smile and say, "well, you asked for it".

The mental pressure on me was increasing because of the absence of accomplishment. To work off the pressure I would go to the gym three times a week and work my heart out for two and a half hours. Apparently I overdid it because in late spring of 1997 I developed a hernia on my right side. Except for 1981-1984, all the years in the US from 1971 to 1997 I never had health insurance.

When a surgeon examined my hernia he also noticed a lemon-sized lump on the left side of my neck. "How long did you have that lump?"

"About 25 years, Doc."

"Well, I can fix your hernia and take out your benign tumor at the same time."

"Doc, how do you know that it is benign?"

"If it was cancerous you would have been dead many times over by now."

"Oh, what a relief."

"Don't worry, your insurance will cover most of it."

"I don't have insurance, Doc."

"Oh, that would be a problem.." the doctor replied.

In September of 1997 someone told me that the Harris County Hospital District offered discounts up to 90% for low income people but you have to be there early because the line gets long quickly. I decided to be the first in line. After work at about 4 AM, I locked the bar, took a shower at home and headed for the HCHD offices. I arrived at 6 AM and no one was around. The doors opened at 8 AM and I was the first to walk in. I presented them my income tax returns of past years and was offered a gold card signifying a 90% discount. Now that I was in possession of the discount card I was able to get assigned to the appropriate hospital without having to pay anything up front! Ben Taub was a teaching hospital and internist Dr. Branford Scott was the head of a team assigned to my case. After a barrage of exams, Friday, February 6, 1998 was set for my double surgery.

When Dr. Scott and his team made the rounds Friday night he noticed that my left side of my neck was somewhat swollen. "It looks like it is being infected. We need to go back in and clean it first thing in the morning." They did just that.

Saturday night Dr. Scott told me that he was glad it was done again, saying "This time we cleaned it up really good." I was sent home after a few days. About a week later, about 1 PM I felt pressure a few inches below where the hernia cut was near my genital area. Pain was added to the pressure and was increasing at an alarming rate. Fortunately, Dr. Scott had given me his cell phone number in order to call him in case of complications so I did. He told me to get to the hospital as soon as possible. A friend of mine dropped me off at about 4 PM; the pain was becoming unbearable. At about 5 PM I was taken upstairs and laid on a bed. Shortly thereafter Dr. Scott and his team along with two other doctors showed up by my bed. One of the new doctors started lightly pressing the area where I was hurting and talking to Dr. Scott. By that time I was vomiting green stuff.

On the way to surgery Dr. Scott asked me if I would prefer another doctor operated on me this time.

"Nope, Dr. Scott, I want you to operate on me again."

The next day when I woke up I felt something on my belly. I looked down and saw a cut in the shape of an L just below my belly button and lots of stitches. Fortunately, all the pain was gone and I was happy.

At night, Dr. Scott and his team came over to check me out. "Paul," Dr. Scott said, "I am glad that you got to the hospital quickly because you were a couple of hours away from being dead. You had a second tear in an area that it is very unusual to have one, so I am sorry we missed it. When we fixed the upper opening the weight of the intestines shifted downwards and some of it slipped through the lower opening. In doing so it got twisted, cutting off the blood flow and they started dying. That's the reason you were vomiting green stuff yesterday afternoon. We had to cut open your belly, cut off the dead part, clean up the area and connect your small intestine before we sewed you up again."

"Now that I have a shorter intestine how will this affect me Dr. Scott?"

"You're not going to miss it, Paul. Your small intestine is about twenty five feet long and we took out only a foot or so. Paul, please let us know when gas passes through."

A couple of days later it did. During that time I was walking like a really old man clutching my side. I was feeling really strong pain in my belly every time I attempted to sit on the commode or tried to get up. I was discharged a few days later.

Sitting in my apartment and feeling that I was recuperating rather fast I began pondering my next move. I felt sick and tired about going into business with partners and friends. I was thinking: "It sure takes a long time to find success but maybe my time hasn't arrived yet. Still, I know it is ahead of me—it shall and will arrive."

Around that time the following phrase came to my attention: "An overnight success takes between 15 and 20 years to materialize".

"Wow," I said, "I can still fit into that definition, if I can come up with at least $50,000 in the bank within the next two years."

I decided that whatever I was going to do next I would do it on my own and with my own money. I didn't care what kind of a job I could get as long as it was legal. Then I started looking at different things.

One day a friend of mine said, "Paul, how about truck driving?"

I winced, recalling what I had said a few years earlier, but when my friend said "They make good money" that grabbed my attention. He went on to explain that the new trucks have improved and been modernized. "As a matter of fact, they call them condos because you can live in them. They are moving living quarters, no need to have an apartment."

I gathered some additional info, made some calculations and decided "Voila, it can be done."

In April 1998 I attended a truck driving school thirty miles south of Dallas, Texas. Talk about grinding gears. Never before had I driven anything with a stick. I joined Werner Enterprises as an OTR (over the road) dry box driver based in Omaha, Nebraska. I chose them because they had a reputation that their training program was the best in the industry and I believe in training. The first two months I teamed up with three different trainers.

From the very beginning I never had a problem planning a trip. The second trainer told me that I can read the US map better than him. "Your only problem is that you grind the gears too hard".

"I need a little bit more time and I'll get the hang of it," I said.

May and June 1998 were training months. In early July I became a solo driver on a 3 month probation and that applies to every new driver. A week later my gear shifting finally became smooth. Since we were paid by the mile (25 cents per qualified mile) I would stop at a truckstop only to get diesel fuel, eat, do my laundry or sleep. The rest of the time you'd find me on the road pushing forward.

A solo driver is required by the company and by law to rest for a minimum of 8 hours for every 10 hours of driving. Werner Enterprises had about 7,500 drivers and their trucks average age was 1.5 years. Their trucks were equipped with satellite dishes. Every fifteen minutes the satellite would pick the location of each truck so our managers would know where we are at any time. In addition, satellite communication was the norm between drivers and their managers. Also the satellite would keep track of our driving hours and alert our managers if we drove beyond the 10 hour limit.

In early October 1998 I became a solo driver in my own right. Around that time I became aware of a trick, from the old timers. This technique let me drive 10 miles without the GPS system being aware of, by pulling over at a precise time and staying still for 4 minutes. But if you pull over twice you gain 20 miles, ten times 100 miles or 20 times you gain 200 miles beyond your 10 hour driving limit. This meant under certain conditions, like pulling a light load (under 20,000 lbs) with no steep hills or mountains to climb it is possible to pull over 20 times per 10 hours of allotted driving time by pulling over every half an hour. Company trucks were equipped with a governor, that meant the maximum speed was 65 miles per hour.

For this trick to work it required you to pull over and stay still for 4 minutes at a precise time, but more than 95% of the time there was no exit available so I had to pull over on the shoulder of the road. That was tedious, cumbersome, sometimes dangerous and against company rules. But since I was at this kind of work for a limited time only, I concluded that the benefits outweighed the risk. I was pulling over every chance I could get during my time as a solo driver. The following two examples illustrate my point.

On November 19, 1998 (my birthday), I wanted to set a record that would be difficult to be matched by anyone else. Early in the morning on that day I left Billings, MT and I arrived at Blue Earth MN. The truck's odometer clocked 839 miles and my satellite clocked 9 hours and 45 minutes. The actual driving time was a little over 13 and a half hours.

On February 27, 1999 the load planners (they do strictly one thing: assign loads to drivers) assigned me to pick up a load from John's Manville in Clebourne, TX and deliver it to Noland Company in New Port News, VA the following Tuesday at 7 AM. I picked up the load on Saturday at 2 PM and delivered it on Monday at 5:30 AM. A little bit after 7 AM Monday morning our load planners called the Noland Company to let them know that their load is scheduled to arrive the next day at 7 AM but they were told "we already received it".

Almost always I was delivering my load well ahead of time. I was late only once for two hours, but because I informed my manager, Wayne Chapman, ahead of time he said: "You did the right thing to let me know in advance, don't worry about it."

I became a trainer in my second year. It is company policy to pay the trainee about $350 a week but the trainer gets paid for miles driven by both the trainer and the trainee. At times our truck was moving for over 20 hours per 24. We would only stop to get fuel and eat.

On July 23, 2000, I picked up a load from Kimberly Clark Company in Fullerton, California and was headed to Hermiston, Oregon traveling north on Interstate 5 when I called my brother Tim Anderson. Tim is a Veterinarian in Bakersville, California.

After a minute of small talk I said, "Tim, I may be a truck driver right now but someday I'll go to Harvard."

Silence, then: "Pantelis, you set an extremely high standard for yourself" (translation: don't bother, you'll never make it to Harvard). It bothered me so I had to respond.

"Tim, I may be reaching for the stars, but my feet are firmly planted on the ground." I am planning a surprise for my brother Tim!!!

I've been to every state of the Union many times over except Vermont. I've either delivered loads to every major city or driven through them. I've driven on every US Interstate, most highways and many back roads day and night. I was fortunate to get to know the physical beauty of our country up close and personal. I marveled at the vastness, variety and the impressive development and how well this Union of 50 different states was put together, yet the boundaries are seamless. It is the only true federal system in the world. I am in awe of our founding fathers foresight, intelligence, political and economic savvy they displayed in constituting the Constitution. I am also thrilled at the devotion we express in upholding the Constitution. We, the United States of America, are so different from the rest of the world, in my opinion, we constitute a world of our own.

In the summer of 2000 a disturbing thought was occupying my mind. For the first time in my life I had a sizeable chunk of money in the bank and I was not worrying how I was going to pay my bills. At times I was trying to rationalize and convince myself that being a truck driver is not really all that bad because it provided me with a peace of mind and allowed me to get to know America up close while putting money in the bank. I was thinking maybe I should stay in it longer than the two year limit I set earlier, which was Christmas 2000.

Every time I would contemplate about staying longer I could feel myself revolt against it. I still had several months ahead of me before I would have to make a decision so, I pressed the pause button for the time being.

In Laredo, Texas, Werner Enterprises had a big, fenced asphalt covered drop yard with an office and a guard-manned gate. The trade with Mexico was increasing and the activity was robust at the drop yard. I've been there several times. As always I was in a hurry to either drop my load at a drop yard or deliver it to a customer asap. That way I would quickly be in line to be assigned a new load.

On Friday September 1, 2000 late in the afternoon, on the long Labor Day weekend, I was approaching Laredo from

Houston (along with another driver, my trainee) from Highway 59 South. I picked up Loop 20 which cuts into I-35. That intersection was undergoing a major construction project and traffic lines were long in every direction. Every time it would take me about 20 minutes to either go through it or make a right turn, pick up I-35 North for about a mile in order to get to the drop yard. Some times I would stay on the two way feeder road in order to reach the drop yard. On that particular Friday though, I saw a sign just before the onramp to I-35 N stating "Feeder Rd closed 1.4 miles". I thought the road to the drop yard is about a mile so I decided to stay on the feeder road.

Unfortunately the road barricade turned out to be placed about 50 feet in front of the road that led to the drop yard. I noticed a small clearing space to my right so I pulled into it in order to make a U turn and go back. The small clearing was surrounded by shrubs about 3 yards tall. At that very moment a jeep with all sides open and 4 passengers on board popped out of the shrubs through a narrow trail. I asked them where that trail led to and they said "Nowhere, you need to go back to Loop 20 find a big parking space to make a U-turn and pick up the onramp to I-35 N". That would delay me in dropping my load for at least an hour and it was getting late already. But, I had no choice so, I took the two way feeder road south.

As I was approaching the on ramp to I-35 N the following thought crossed my mind: "How about if I just pass it, then make a U-turn." So as soon as I passed the onramp I noticed a spot of the feeder road that was a bit wider. I pulled to the edge and stopped. It took less than a minute to realize that I could indeed make a U turn. At that very moment I saw the jeep, which was just ahead of me, make a U turn, now facing North and it stopped.

"How nice of them," I thought, "they're blocking the north bound traffic so I could make the U turn which I completed within less than 30 seconds and headed back for the onramp to I-35 N.

While I was still on the ramp and picking up speed my trainee said, "Paul, those people in the Jeep are looking at our truck in a funny way."

I looked and saw all 4 of them with their necks stretched, looking with intense amazement at our truck as if they wanted to read something. Every truck has a 5 digit ID #. I felt a bit uncomfortable as this was out of the ordinary and I couldn't make sense of it.

"Well, I worry about nothing, they probably are amazed as to how quickly I made the U turn on a dime."

Early part of the following week I received a somewhat cryptic message from Wayne Chapman, my manager: "Safety wants me to bring you in, but I'll take my time."

Wow, that didn't sound good. I knew that U turns on feeder roads were against company rules. Did those people in the jeep report me to the company? Well, if that was the case I decided to face the music. And so on Friday September 8, 2000, I returned to the Omaha terminal.

Monday morning, September 11, 2000, I was told that the director of the Safety department wants to see me. The director was in his mid-30s and was less than a month on the job. The first thing he said to me when I entered his office was, "Did you make a U turn on a feeder road in Laredo, Texas?"

"Yes sir, I did, in less than 30 seconds and no one was in danger."

"It doesn't matter, I have a stack this high of accidents happening when drivers attempt to make U turns on feeder roads of a freeway. It costs the company 7.5 million a year to insure itself and U turns on feeder roads are a big chunk of it. The number one reason for a driver to get fired by the company is when he makes an illegal U turn. I need you to place your ID card on my desk."

I said "Sir, I promise I will not do it ever again."

"Nope," he said and opened the company's manual.

He pointed to the sentence that stated in bold letters: "The number one reason for a driver to get fired is when he makes a U turn on a feeder road of a freeway."

"I am afraid that I'll have to let you go."

Up to that point I thought that I was doing them a favor working for the company, but this conversation made it clear to me that all this production I created for the company was not appreciated and that irked me. "Maybe this is a blessing in disguise," I thought, and promptly placed my ID card on his desk and walked out. I rented a car and headed for Houston, TX.

I went to visit Mohamed Alam, an old friend of mine. Five months earlier he had purchased a 14 year old business for $120,000. His business included Vehicle State Inspection, chip rock repair, detailing and renting out U-Hall vehicles to customers. I hanged out at his business for 2-3 days, observing his operation. The State Inspection caught my eye, I saw potential. "Recession proof" glared at me, it is state mandated, regardless of economic conditions.

Some states do emissions testing of their vehicles by themselves. The state of Texas though allows the private sector to participate in the following way. It is a two step process. First, an entrepreneur applies for certification and picks a location. The Department of Public Safety approves the location as an inspection station. Second, the DPS certifies 3 vendors so the entrepreneur can choose one of the 3 to buy the hardware and software they need for their business. The entrepreneur studies the DPS manual, takes a written and practical test and if he passes, the DPS gives its final approval by issuing a certificate and a badge to him so he can open for business. Once a month, a DPS representative shows up at the location and checks out the paperwork to see if everything is done according to DPS rules and regulations. Entrepreneurs buy books of stickers in advance from the DPS, that's how the state makes its money and the owner keeps the inspection fee, which is set by the DPS.

"Mohamed," I said, "how about if we go 50-50 on a new location."

"Sure, go find one and we'll sign a one year lease. If we don't make it we'll move into another location."

I knew just where to look at—in the suburb of Kingwood. Ever since April of 1982 I had this secret wish to someday live there. It is a residential enclave like no other anywhere in the US and I've been just about everywhere. It is a master planned residential development comprised of about 26 villages. Houses and streets (with green trails) are imbedded in a real forest. It is also known as the "Livable Forest" and they don't call it KINGWOOD for nothing.

Constantine Nicolaidis was the second Greek student I met back in 1971 and he happened to live in Templin Hall at that time. In April 1982 my then wife Sandy and I ran into him at the Greek church one Sunday. He told me that he and his wife recently bought half a million 2 story house by the golf course in a beautiful Houston suburb called Kingwood, about 30 miles north and east of downtown Houston. He offered to take us to his house to meet his wife and show us around. Well, the favorable impression went to my head and stayed there.

I searched this area thoroughly for a week. The villages have very strict deed restrictions. There was no free standing building available so it had to be in a shopping strip. Unfortunately every shopping strip owner I talked to didn't want to hear about anything that was automotive. Running out of chances to find a spot I felt sad and somewhat depressed, so I drove around behind a big shopping mall to take a break and collect my thoughts. There was a small shopping strip hidden behind the large one. I got out of my car to stretch my legs when I noticed a 4"x6" piece of paper taped to the inside of the last front door of the small shopping strip.

I approached the front door to read the note. "On September 30th we will be moving to 1700 Northpark" (one of the main streets in Kingwood)". I noticed an overhead door on the side of the building, same level with the ground. This was perfect for cars entering inside, I wouldn't have to remove a ramp. A real estate firm was anchoring the strip so I asked them for the landlord's phone # which I got plus the key to the empty space. Within two minutes I decided it was the perfect place even though it was hidden and I didn't know if the landlord would agree to lease it for an automotive business.

When I called the next day I was told that the landlord was out of the country and I should call back at the end of October. Excited about the spot I urged my friend Mohamed to let me show it to him. Finally, a couple weeks later on a Sunday afternoon we arrived at the spot. Mohamed got out of his car and I can tell he is not happy. He looks east and west then said: "Where is the traffic?" Trying to break the ice by being funny I raise my right arm and pointed over the back wall of the large shopping center saying "on the other side of this wall." He looked at me and said: "This is a dead spot, I am not interested, find another spot."

I couldn't go back to the drawing board. I had $62,000 in the bank when I left Werner Enterprises and by now I had $55,000. I was afraid that if my funds dropped below $50,000 I might not be able to finance my new venture with my own money. With my kind of credit, I couldn't borrow a dime. So, this location would have to work out for me.

I returned to my apartment some 45 miles away depressed. I counted on Mohamed because he knew the business and I knew nothing about it, his credit was very good (I had none) and the most important thing, he had an established business, so the landlord would be more inclined to lease a space to him. I fell in love with that spot, it was inside Kingwood where I always wanted to be and I liked the layout. So what if it was hidden, I would make people come to me! My mind was circling the spot even though I hadn't talked to the landlord yet.

I couldn't sleep so at about 2:30 AM Monday Morning I said to myself: "I really don't need Mohamed's help, I'll handle it myself, it can't be rocket science." I just needed to ask Cammie's opinion. This lady was working at the new house finding office in the front of Kingwood. I used to stop by when I was scouring the area for a spot and chat with her, get some coffee and a copy of the local newspaper.

Early Monday I walked into her office and said, "Cam, do you know where Clear Pool is located behind Stein Mart? I am thinking of leasing that spot for a vehicle State Inspection business. It is kinda hidden, so do you think people would come?"

She paused and said, "Paul, if you let them know where you are and provide them with good service then they will." A piece of cake, I could do that. And so, it took a test marketing of one person to confirm what I had a gut feeling for.

A few days later I met with Mr. Mehdi Sharifian, the landlord, at his office. Initially he showed some hesitation but I promised him I would work hard, provide good service and keep the space clean. Finally he said, "I only need one month's rent of $1300 as a security deposit."

I asked and received a one year lease with two 3 year options and the whole agreement was subject to the DPS approving my space as an inspection station. Also, I got free rent until January 15, 2001 in order to get all the necessary approvals from the DPS and have time to remodel the space.

On Monday November 20'th, 2000 I signed the lease. At the time I lived near Almeda Mall and to get to Kingwood I needed to drive about 45 miles one way. The next day I arrived at my future business location at 8 AM in order to wait for a DPS technician to show up. My phone service was already activated.

At about 11 AM the phone rang. Liz, my landlord's secretary, tells me that Mr. Sharifian wanted to talk to me. This didn't sound good to me.

"Paul," the landlord said, "the tenants of the shopping center found out about your business and they don't want you there. Charlie, the lady next door, threatened to sue me! I don't want to have problems with the rest of the tenants so please come back and I'll give you back your security deposit, unless you make a deal with Charlie."

My knees felt weak, my body trembled a bit and my throat got dry. "Oh God, when will this test end? What else can I do?" I did have a signed lease, but I couldn't afford to get involved in litigation with my landlord.

"I am very sorry to hear this, Mr. Sharifian" I managed to say. I hung up and headed for the door. The door closed behind me and I was standing on my left leg, my right leg moving forward towards the direction of my parked car. With my right foot still off the ground I suddenly made a sharp right turn towards the entrance door of my neighbor Charlie.

"I can't let this spot slip away, I've got to hang on to it." I told myself I would talk and make a deal with Charlie. I knocked on the entrance door of her business and her assistant Suzette guided me inside where Charlie was eating lunch and her children Elliott (13) and Cameron (9) were playing some kind of game.

"Hi Charlie, I am Paul Rachman, I understand you have some concerns about my business. I would like to explain what I am planning to do, describe my business and see if we can find common ground to the benefit of both of us."

"No, no, no I can't take a chance. Some of my clients have cancer and come here to cleanse their intestines. I don't want exhaust fumes to seep through the walls into my place." She owned a colonoscopy business.

"Charlie, it won't be a garage. We will not fix, replace or adjust anything. It will be strictly a State Inspection, in and out quickly. The vehicle will run between half a minute to a couple minutes only, and I will take the fumes outside the building by utilizing special tubes."

At that very moment my cell phone rang and I went outside to answer it. It was Liz saying "Mr. Sharifian asked me to call DPS, which I did, and I asked them if they would have a problem approving my location and they said it shouldn't be a problem." I felt encouraged that my landlord took the trouble to inquire.

When I walked back in again I saw a facial transformation in Charlie. Before the call she was feisty, now she looked calm. "Paul, my children liked you and they asked me to make a deal with you. I guess this is your lucky day."

"Thank you kids" I said with great relief. "Well Charlie, what can I do for you?"

"I need to get more space from you Paul, about 7-8 feet deep and 35 feet wide. I thought I had extra space, I could accommodate her plus my rent would go down proportionately.
"I'll be happy to do that Charlie, since my rent will go down."

"Oh no, she said, you will continue to pay the rent, or no deal."

"Charlie, that's not fair, I'm giving you a part of my space so you should assume the rent."

I knew she was taking advantage of me, but my eyes were glued to the prize. "Charlie, I have limited funds. I can do it for 3 months only."

"Nope, not enough" she said.
"Alright Charlie, this is my final offer, 5 months or I'll go belly up."
"I'll take it" she said. Immediately, I called my landlord to inform him that I made a deal with Charlie. Now that I knew I was going to hang onto my space it was time to deal with the DPS.
In the morning of January 18, 2001 the DPS issued its final approval and State Inspection of Kingwood opened for business as a start up! During the remainder of January I inspected 3 cars, one of which was my landlord's who came over from some 30 miles away. In February I did 17 inspections but in March and April I did 137 and 289 respectively. My break-even point at

the time was at about 240 inspections a month. I made a little profit in my 4th month in business and never looked back. I reached the 500 a month inspection mark by September of 2001 and the 600 mark by April of 2002. On May 1, 2002 I had to upgrade the inspection test with new hardware and software as mandated by the DPS. The cost of the upgrade was about $45,000. For the first 20 months I was a one man company, working 7 days a week 360 days a year. During that time I placed 15,000 reminder cards on people's cars that their sticker either already expired or was due this month or the next.

By September of 2002 I felt exhausted so I hired my first employee. He quit four months later to become a paramedic. I went through more than half a dozen employees to finally settle on Jim Lucenti on August 2003. He took an early retirement from Exxon and was looking for something to do. A very dependable person, Jim is honest and a hard worker. Today, I have two employees. We are hovering at about 900-1000 inspections per month. Every year we're doing more inspections than the last.

In October of 2004 I bought from a customer of mine and in an excellent condition a 1995 Lexus LS400, my dream car. For two years I was checking the newspaper for an LS400 with black exterior, tan leather interior, golden letters, sunroof, one owner, garage kept, tinted windows and at a good price. My Lexus came with all of the above plus it came equipped with a radar detector.

A month later I became a shareholder of Partners Bank of Texas, a brand new bank. Three and a half years later Sterling bank bought PBT and I tripled my initial investment.

In late 2004 my landlord spent $85,000 at my request to build a brand new 1000 square foot building to accommodate my increased business. My landlord is now very happy that I am doing so well. He once mentioned to me that the reason he asked me for only one month's rent at the beginning as a security deposit was because he didn't think that I was going to make it. He was not the only one. My new DPS lady/tech once said to my employee Jim Lucenti that when she was first assigned to our area she had trouble finding our location and her initial impression was that I was not going to make it.

On February 5, 2005 I bought my brand new 2 story house with a $32,500 down payment and a $118,704 first loan at 5.5% fixed interest rate. Also in 2005 I installed a Superflow high performance DYNO in the new building to measure horsepower and torque of race cars. After almost two years it became apparent to me that I tried to bite more than I could chew so I sold the equipment to a guy in Pasadena, Texas. I lost some money but I'm glad I tried it because a "what if" question would have bugged me the rest of my life. Sticking to your core business lies the secret to a sustainable business success.

Years 2005, 2006 and 2007 were good and each year was better than the previous one. In 2007 the presidential race got underway and I kept a close eye on it. I remember blurting out, "Hey, that's where I am from too" when I heard for the very first time that President Obama's grandparents were from El Dorado, Kansas. In 2008 I invested with the Walton International Group, Atlas Energy Resources and again in a start up bank called Plains State Bank. On April 1, 2009 I paid off my home mortgage in 4 years flat (no April Fools!)

I feel blessed being the owner of a very successful business. Mr. Harold Frank would be proud of me, I hope he is still alive. This is what America is all about. A land full of promise and opportunity; "The Promised Land". Promise and opportunity cannot be given. They are out there, they must be pursued relentlessly, regardless of the resources on hand. That's the entrepreneurial spirit of America where through innovation miracles do happen.

People need to be thankful and appreciative of their country, the United States of America. Through its Constitution it guarantees its members "Life, Liberty and the Pursuit of Happiness".

The people who are unappreciative and blame this great country for their shortcomings do this because they incorrectly read the Constitution as "Life, Liberty and Happiness". They omit the crucial word "Pursuit" which implies "chase" which in turn implies "risk of failure" and failure is an integral part of success. It is the other side of the same coin, they go together in a ratio of about 10 to 1, ten attempts to one success. We also observe this ratio in the jungles of Africa: ten chases, one kill.

That is when perseverance kicks in and keeps you going failure after failure until you reach that magical point called "success" and the achievers are identified. "Survival of the fittest": It is the natural law that the fittest thrive and the rest just survive. Do you want to thrive? Well, get fit! You achieve happiness through achievement, it is the only true and enduring happiness. Some people might say "we're human and rules of the animal kingdom don't apply to us". Well, not so fast. The Theory of Everything and fractal geometry (Benoit Mandelbrot) suggest that nature, at its most fundamental level, uses simple rules (blueprints if you will) that produce this incredible variety and complexity that appear to us as chaos, yet patterns can be observed and where patterns are present order exists. Thus, we can infer that order exists even in chaos. An example would be, "The blueprint of a tree is the same as that of the forest". If nature would have had a separate blueprint for every little bitty thing that wouldn't have been very efficient, but we know that nature is unimaginably efficient.

Everything around us is made of star dust: stars, planets, rocks, trees, water, metals, animals and humans are made of atoms and they come in 92 flavors. All this variety and complexity is the result of different combinations of those atoms. Since atoms obey their own strange laws, there is inter-connectivity in their output. Our DNA is similar to that of the animal kingdom, so if 10 to 1 applies to the jungle it also applies to us. Besides, we do say "it's a jungle out there" because there is truth to it, it is the law of nature.

If one word could describe America that word would be INNOVATION. As Elon Musk, of Tesla Motors & Space X, very appropriately once stated in a February 09 article in GQ: "America is where people like me need to go. That is where people like me have always gone. It is as true now as it has always been. Funny how people seem to have forgotten that."

The reason? "Almost all innovation in the world takes place in the United States."

Innovation in thinking got us out of the caves and innovation brought us science and technology. Innovation is the link, a pathway if you will, between us and our creator. God gave us a brain so we can develop the intelligence needed to explore (and simultaneously benefit) the pathway to our creator. We humans have created nothing original. The elements of our civilization were already embedded in nature. All we did was discover them (through innovation) and combined them in a certain way to meet our needs and benefit mankind. So, please America, do not stifle innovation for any reason. **It is America's destiny and duty to be at the forefront of innovation for the benefit of all mankind.**

Innovation is almost transparent; it does not bring immediate benefit. So, in an economic downturn it is the first one to suffer, unfortunately. It shows how imperfect we humans are.

Innovation got us out of the caves and the dark ages, yet we slash or postpone funding for R&D when we need it most.

Economic downturns take place in two distinct ways. The first and most common one is a cyclical one. The peaks and valleys are relatively smooth and cover several years each. But the second one is sudden, imminent and its impact rattles the system to its foundation. Potentially catastrophic is the word used at times. The heart (Wall Street) suffers a heart attack and stops pumping oxygen and nutrient rich blood to the brain and other organs. Open heart surgery is needed asap. If successful, then a variety of medicines, a strict diet and regular check ups needed for life to make sure there will be no repeat. What could be the cause of all this? The answer is simple & clear. Systematic, wide spread and unchecked FRAUD. It is an economic crime, and it is a "**Net Negative**", that must be attacked and stamped out from our economic system. The time has come for the government to do the right thing, that is to implement President Truman's advice to "deliver some quick kicks into the right asses."

The damaging impact of fraud spreads far beyond people losing their houses, their jobs and companies starving for credit. It stifles innovation, and that's the biggest crime of all.

But who really brings innovation to market? Certainly NOT the government. It is the American companies: small, medium and large that, through their innovation have created the American economic folklore that the rest of the world is envious of. Of course, government was a catalyst by providing, at times, the appropriate environment. So what went wrong?

Well, here is my take. There is an overwhelming concentration of economic power on Wall Street. We know that absolute power corrupts absolutely. Our founding fathers realized that so, they implemented checks and balances on our government.

Well, how about if we implement checks & balances on Wall Street, **now**. I wonder if the Wall Street banks were partnerships, instead of being corporations, would they engage in predatory, reckless, irresponsible and unconscionable practices? We should have listened to Brooksley Born.

Wall Street is not the only source of this financial crisis. The toothless and clawless regulatory system, a timid Federal Reserve along with some governmental policies have allowed this financial hiccup to be morphed into a hurricane. But this is a subject for another time, or perhaps another book.

America allows you to grow, blossom and become all you can be, if you pay the price. Your development is limited only by your imagination, persistence and passion.

At the end, it was all worth it. Privileged, gratitude and indebtedness to America run deeply inside me. There is only one thing missing, a family of my own, but something had to give. Following Sam Walton's advice: "The absence of debt magnifies opportunity", I owe nothing to no one and have no credit cards (on purpose). I have only a debit card but plenty of cash. I take great pleasure when I throw offers of credit into the waste basket.

It's a real privilege to be born a US citizen. It provides real and significant advantages. In my opinion, anyone who is born a US citizen is like being born with a silver spoon in their mouth. Please, do not complain if someone else's silver spoon is bigger than yours, please be thankful that you got one.

EMBASSY OF THE
UNITED STATES OF AMERICA

Belgrade, Yugoslavia

May 19, 1980

Mr. Paul Pantelis Rachmanides
Diaki CBS AEBE
Syngrou 19
P.O. Box 2533
Makriyianni, Athens 403
Greece

Dear Mr. Rachmanides:

Thank you for your letter of May 9, 1980. It is very unusual
to receive news from someone who received a visa such a
long time ago.

I am glad to know that you were so successful in your studies
and are doing well in your career.

I have no present plans to return to Thessaloniki, but I wish
you well on your assignment to that very pleasant city. Thank
you again for taking the trouble to write to me.

Sincerely,

John G. Peters
American Consul

CBS
INTERNATIONAL S.A.

7442/12/2651

31 August 1974

Dear Mr. _____,

Further to our conversations I write to offer you a position on the following terms:

a. The position is that of Executive Trainee, to be confirmed after satisfactory completion of a six month trial period. You will be available for duty anywhere in Europe.

b. Starting date will be as soon as possible in September 1974. Our personnel department in New York will provide you with a ticket from _____ to Paris. CBS will pay for up to 20 kilos overweight.

c. Your basic salary will be F7000 a month gross, before the usual social security deductions. Your first assignment will be in Brussels, and an allowance for living in temporary quarters may be decided if local management think justified. Your salary will be reviewed after 6 months.

d. If at the end of 6 months you or we decide not to continue, we would provide you with an air ticket to Athens.

If you are in agreement kindly sign the attached copy.

We are glad that you have chosen CBS for a career.

Sincerely,

117

August 13, 1960

Mr. Odl Schbandis   c.c. Peter de Rougemont
Managing Director
CBS Records, Greece
Athens, 803

Dear Mr. Schbandis:

I have been with CBS Records International for eight months and with CBS
Greece for about three months. I have found my position in the music
industry exciting, interesting, and challenging. I am particularly proud
of the fact that I have been for eleven months part of an organization
that sets the standards for the industry.

However, personal considerations compel me, with a heavy heart, to inform
you that I would like August 5 to mark the end of our employment agreement.
I would be happy to stay for a 10 day period starting today through
August 13, 1960 if this is desired by the company.

I realize that by coming to this decision I am forfeiting good challenges,
opportunities and rewards. It is the hardest decision I have ever had to
make. I only hope that it is the right one.

Sincerely yours,

PAUL RASMUSSEN

to Mr. Ed Moore
   Mr. Paul Russell

DISKI CBS AEBE

19 .... Ave.
P.O. Box 203 Maroussi
Athens 48 - Greece
(01) 93 206069 - 93 37 913
Telex: 23228 CBSR GR
Cable: COLRECORD

Sol Rabinowitz, Managing Director

C O N F I D E N T I A L

Dear Paul,

I was sorry to receive your letter dated August 21, which was
obviously written July 23. Both Costas Nikitas and I feel
that you could have had a successful career with our company,
and regret your leaving.

I, of course, respect your decision and wish you well in
your future endeavors.

We thank you and accept your offer to remain in your present
capacity until August 15, 1980. Please advise Mr. Nikitas
if you would prefer to leave sooner should we find a replacement
at an earlier date.

Again, good luck, and I also hope your decision was the right
one.

Sincerely yours,

Sol Rabinowitz

July 24, 1980

Koll Center - Newport
4500 MacArthur Boulevard
Newport Beach, California 92660
Telephone (714) 955-1146

SEARCHMASTERS, INC.

June 15, 1981

Mr. Paul N. Rachmanides
4600 N. Oak Avenue 41
Glendale, Arizona 85301

Dear Paul:

It was nice of you to drive up to visit with me. I enjoyed meeting you very
much. As I mentioned, we do not have a search assignment which fits your
background. I will keep your resume in the file should something develop.

You might be interested in meeting a fellow young Greek American who married a
girl from Greece a year or so ago. He is well connected with the Greek
community here and owns a profitable handyman/watch mobile home services. I
told him about you and he said he would enjoy meeting you.

Steve Katsipianis
26132 Via de Toledo
San Juan Capistrano, California 92675

Please keep me informed as your career progresses.

Sincerely,

Harold R. Grant, Ph.D.
Vice President

HRG/rm

My parents in West Germany in the mid 70's.

Me sliding across the rope.

Same aerobridge from a different angle.

Ranger school graduation ceremony May 1970.

Graduating from Paratrooper school October 30'th, 1970.

After finding the three bear cubs.

As Second Lieutenant in April 1971.

Jill Anderson, my little sister in the 1970s.

My dad Andy Anderson and me in the late 1970's.

From left to right: Tim, Mom and Mark paying me a visit in May 2007.

My website address for contacting:
http://www.publishedauthors.net/paulrachman/index.html